TOO BUSY TO DIE

TOO BUSY TO DIE

My Declarations of Independence

FRANCES LIEF NEER

Note for Librarians: a cataloguing record for this book that includes Dewey Classification and US Library of Congress numbers is available from the National Library of Canada. The complete cataloguing record can be obtained from the National Library's online database at: www.nlc-bnc.ca/amicus/index-e.html

ISBN 1-4120-2526-5

TRAFFORD

This book was published on-demand in cooperation with Trafford Publishing.
On-demand publishing is a unique process and service of making a book available for retail sale to the public taking advantage of on-demand manufacturing and Internet marketing. On-demand publishing includes promotions, retail sales, manufacturing, order fulfilment, accounting and collecting royalties on behalf of the author.

Suite 6E, 2333 Government St., Victoria, B.C. V8T 4P4, CANADA

Phone	250-383-6864	Toll-free 1-888-232-4444 (Canada & US)	
Fax	250-383-6804	E-mail sales@trafford.com	

Web site www.trafford.com TRAFFORD PUBLISHING IS A DIVISION OF TRAFFORD HOLDINGS LTD.

Trafford Catalogue #04-0354 www.trafford.com/robots/04-0354.html

10 9 8 7 6 5 4 3 2 1

To Christine, Dolly, and Kirk,
Who sustain and guide me
Through my dark days

And to all those I may have hurt
I make amends

To thine own self be true,
And it must follow, as the night the day,
Thou canst not then be false to any man.
—Shakespeare

Life is a banquet, and most poor
sons of bitches are starving to death.
—Auntie Mame

TABLE OF CONTENTS

Foreword

To me, Frances Lief Neer is a study in contrasts. Sentimental and profane. Kind and prickly by turns. Physically diminished, but passionate in spirit. She's in the winter of her life, yet has a quality of spring. A new bud pushing up defiantly through the hard tundra of circumstance. Frances is an old woman whose child is still so much a part of her.

I've known her barely a year and am thankful for the privilege.

When I'm with her I have to keep reminding myself that Frances is blind. Strangely, she seems to have visual focus. And I've come to believe that although she doesn't know what I look like, Frances "sees" me. "Are you standing?" she'll ask, hinting that she wants me to sit down with her. When I do she looks toward the sound of my voice, a little more relaxed, satisfied that we're on the same level.

Her smile is wonderfully mischievous, that of a born prankster. When I met her, I was expecting a generational limitation of what we might have in common. Frances quickly dispelled that notion when she told me that once she had put an ad in a newspaper for male companionship. "Do you know what SWF in one of those ads means?" she asked me.

"Uh… single white female, I think."

"No. Sexy, will fuck." Then she smiled teasingly. "So they say, anyway."

In that moment I knew I'd met a kindred soul.

When the reaper eventually comes knocking at her door, Frances no doubt will "see" him too. She'll wave him off with irritation while she takes another phone call, records a new thought, helps someone with her gentle encouragement. The grim fellow might as well just set his scythe against the wall and wait his turn. Frances will be chin deep in the business of living.

—Paul Samuelson, a friend of recent standing.

Preface

Just after the change of millennium, I turned eighty-six. My earliest memory, when I was three, was perched on my father's shoulders watching the Armistice Day parade in New York City at the end of World War I. Two of the marching doughboys home from the war were my oldest brothers. "MIKE! AARON! I'M HERE, I'M HERE!" I shouted. Of course, they must not have been able to hear me, nor I able to see them in the seemingly endless phalanxes of soldiers. But I can't remember for sure. It was so long ago. So very long ago.

Bearing in mind the words of my friend Kirk Phillips, "Life is as fragile as a bubble," I look back on my memories and experiences with increased appreciation. By now, I have the glorious opportunity of perspective. I can finally laugh at tired old travails, celebrate successes, understand foolish acts, and forgive myself for throwing away chances. I'm happy even though I'm blind. I love my fellow man, although I must admit there are some I can do without. Since my late seventies I have written three books, the one you hold in your hand is my fourth. I want to share with you my excitements and the drive to meet the challenges that confront me.

Most of the time these days I am in my executive position, stretched out on my couch with a couple of tape recorders at my fingertips, as well as a radio and telephone. I read books in Braille and listen to them on tape. I've been facilitating a monthly low vision forum at a nearby medical center for more than fifteen years. My phone is a hotline.

How I got to this point is a long story, so I may as well just dive in, peeling back the layers of my private life and my public, professional one. Let the quips fall where they may. I'll sweep them all up into a basket of heartbreaks and happiness.

There are many beginnings in a lifetime, but only one ending. And I'm just too damn busy to get to it.

TOO BUSY TO DIE

PART 1

EAST COAST—FOR BETTER OR FOR WORSE

Growing up in Rockaway

The sand, the surf, the sky, the sun. The boom of the waves crashing on the shore. The cool foam of the tide sliding up the beach and around my feet and ankles on warm summer days. This was just beyond my front door where I grew up in Rockaway Beach, Long Island. It was the closest thing to heaven on earth I could imagine then, or still now. This place by the sea was the joy and magic of freedom.

It was also my refuge.

I was born when my mother was forty-five. After motherhood with five male children, along I came twelve years after the last son—a girl. When I was growing up she complimented me for exemplary schoolwork, but never showed pleasure in just my being. I soon realized that hugs I would give her were never returned. My father was more attentive to me.

My sixth year was the happiest and most comfortable time of my life. That was when I felt most secure. But my fantasia came to an abrupt halt at age six. Suddenly, in my own family I sensed I was *persona non grata.*

Four of my five brothers had married, set up their own homes, and were starting families. My youngest brother Harry was a dozen years my senior, and my father and mother were old enough to be my grandparents. Between my chattering sisters-in-law and the arrival of the first of their cute little babies, where was I? In limbo. My heretofore happy, secure life dissolved into uncertainties. I straddled my brothers' generation and that of their children, closer to the latter but belonging neither to one group nor the other. I was accepted, but no longer celebrated.

expectation to be celebrated

As for my little nieces and nephews, I accepted them, but was not inclined to cuddle or play with them. They were simply there, facts of my existence. How could I rejoice in their babyhood and toddler cuteness when I myself was rarely hugged, kissed, or caressed? I didn't have much of an idea what that felt like. It took many years before my own then twenty-year-old daughter Amy made me realize that I'd never known what affectionate mothering could be.

When I was still a little girl, my brothers and their wives paid some attention to me, but that was probably due in part to my usefulness as a child model for their imminent parenthood. Soon our house was crawling with my nieces and nephews, all only a few years younger than I. And all receiving more beaming smiles. I was alone in a crowd.

Aside from my days of refuge at the beach, I did have some good childhood times at home. Despite a hole in my young heart, I also have some precious memories of my family when I was little.

An early recollection is of leaning backward against a piano bench, clutching the sides for balance, and straining to reach the pumps on the behemoth that was the family player piano. I couldn't reach the pumps sitting forward, but I could reach and push them as long as I was stretched out backward on the

2

bench, holding on for dear life. Whatever music roll was already set into it was good enough for me; I was delighted with any melody that came out.

One song that I particularly liked was the then-popular "When Francis Dances With Me." My brother Jack bounced me around to that tune, even though the "Franc*is*" sung about was a young man. But it was as if that song was written just for me when Jack took some liberty with the lyrics.

> *When Frances dances with me, golly gee,*
> *I'm as gay as can be.*
> *There is no question it's dancing we love;*
> *She fits in my arms like a motorman's glove.*
>
> *I wear a tuxedo and, my, how it fits.*
> *I look like the head waiter up at the Ritz.*
> *And she wears a gown that's got twenty-eight slits*
> *When Frances dances with me.*

The lock on the piano keys could be released so that the keys danced by themselves along with the sound. To me, that was wondrous, and whenever that song played I was in my private reverie. With all the singing going on in this large family of brothers, wives, and girlfriends, that was my song.

I woke up on Christmas morning that year to find a roll of shiny pennies and a kitten in my crib. It was probably Jack's idea. He was a darling fellow, full of kindness and zip. I liked the pennies, but really didn't want a cat in my cradle. I remember my brother Aaron sitting with me on the kitchen floor, playing with my new wooden trains. He liked them so much I hardly

3

recall having much chance to play with them myself. I was able to enjoy my French doll, though, a gift from my brother Joe and his wife Rose.

When I was growing up, my brothers would always come with their wives and children to our home in Belle Harbor for the Christmas holidays. My oldest brother Mike would dress up as Santa Claus, which caused his own little baby boy to bawl with fright. Mike would burst in with a "HO-HO-HO!" and an enormous bag of gifts. We had no Christmas tree but the children were delighted and the grownups had a fine time visiting.

After a big meal, prepared by my mother and her daughters-in-law, the women would clean up and take care of the babies, while the men would retire upstairs, each to a separate bedroom, for an afternoon snooze.

There was also happiness in the birthday parties my mother put on for me. They were essentially parties for the adults, however, with few children involved. The first one I recall was on my fourth birthday. "Frances," Ma said to me, "You're having a birthday party and everyone is going to bring you presents."

When the time came, I quivered excitedly at the door and asked the guests as they arrived, "Did you bring me a present?"

My mother looked at me in embarrassment, saying, "Just listen to her, asking for gifts!"

Why is it wrong to ask for my presents? I thought. *Didn't she say people would be bringing them to me?*

Some years later, my mother began work on a beribboned bouquet of sugar cubes, adding one cube per birthday. This special bouquet was set in the china closet, not to be touched from year to year until my

4

birthday came around. This custom probably goes back to the early 1800s in Eastern Europe. I was sentimental enough to create just such a bouquet of beribboned sugar cubes for my granddaughter Christine on her sixteenth birthday, held together at the top by my mother's wedding ring.

One time, my brother Joe took me to the circus. I rode on an elephant, and I clearly recollect what it felt like to tentatively touch that gnarled hide. He showed me a woman who had no arms or legs, and yet could jump down from her chair. Joe was the storyteller of the family. He was always patient with me.

My father would take me to the movies. I saw Charlie Chaplin and Jackie Coogan in *The Kid*. I especially liked Jackie. I figured we were about the same age, so felt a kinship with him. My father also took me to see *Shoulder Arms*, another Chaplin film in which Charlie couldn't find his way out of the woods because the trees kept moving around him. Then there was a movie starring Pearl White. In one scene, unbeknownst to her, she was in a dangerous situation. As she sat at her vanity, combing her long tresses, a figure stealthily approached her from behind. I was so frightened I closed my eyes, and never did find out what happened to Pearl.

Dad would tuck me into my crib every night, telling me stories from *The Red Pocketbook*. But though he was attentive to me, my father's favorite child was my niece Shirley, a good-natured, blue-eyed, blond toddler to whom he lost his heart.

One Easter, when I was about ten, the house was full of sisters-in-law and infants—a bustle of young women and Ma cooking and jabbering away. I was an incidental. I spent a great deal of time with my nose buried in books.

I was sick and tired of my sister-in-law Estelle's strident tones and her constantly bawling baby boy Elliot. Even reading didn't serve as escape, so I closed my book, put my glasses on the dining room buffet, and ran out of the house to get away from all the noise. I came back later to find that Estelle had plopped little Elliot smack on top of my glasses.

"Hey, my glasses are broken!" I cried.

"Well, you shouldn't leave them on the buffet," Estelle snapped.

I didn't bother saying that it seemed to me the glasses belonged there more than her baby.

My nephew Bert took an interest in my Boy Scout manual and my box of oil paints, so I gave them to him. For this, I received thanks not from Bert nor from his mother or father. Not from anyone. That was just the way things were.

My sister-in-law Ethel and I went to see *The Phantom of the Opera*, with Lon Chaney. It was scary for a young child, and later on at home, when it was time for me to go upstairs to bed, Ethel teased me cruelly. "The phantom may be up there," she said. This shriveled my heart. Everybody laughed, and it took some deep breaths for me to go upstairs alone in the dark. My mother never protected and comforted me at times like these.

My sister-in-law Rose felt a great need to direct and correct me. Rose was a reasonable and deeply intelligent person, except when it came to overindulging her child. I was scolded by her for objecting to her toddler Doris running into my room and upsetting my things.

expectations of the way her large family should have treated her

"Why does she have to play in *my* room?" I asked.

"She has to run around, doesn't she?" replied Rose. There was no thought of closing the door so the little girl couldn't get in. I was the one considered unreasonable.

Once, when I was in high school, Rose said to me in front of my mother, "Why don't you wash your *own* silk stockings, Frances? Why does Mama have to do that for you?"

I didn't answer, but thought, *I'd get around to doing it. But if Ma's already at the basin, and wants to wash my stockings, why not let her do it?* But there was no use in actually saying this. No one was much interested in my opinions.

My brother Joe faulted me because I wouldn't give his little girl a book I loved, but which she wanted. "Give the baby that book, will you?"

"It's *my* book. Harry gave it to *me*."

"You can read another one."

"No," I protested. "I want to keep my own book."

"You're a selfish child!" Joe said, disgusted.

I stuck to my guns. Harry had given me *Now We Are Six* by A.A. Milne, and I refused to give it up. I'd rather be considered "selfish" than be taken advantage of.

My sisters-in-law, like my mother, were homemakers of the old school, and their formal education was limited. Their ideas of child rearing probably resembled that of their mothers, grandmothers, and great grandmothers: a disproportionate blend of concern for their children's behavior and food intake, with not much time for fun and games.

As I grew older, I failed to fit the established patterns of the female family members, or that of their

In contrast to the women in her family — negative view of women

social milieu. I was a serious student, and developed into an <u>independent thinker</u>. I earned my own way through college, the first of the women in my family to seek higher education. I became politically aware. Many in my family, especially the women, disapproved of me because I didn't conform to familial habits or expectations. <u>I was left to fight my way out of my own bag</u>, and I became somewhat of a maverick.

Whatever I didn't get at home, I sought out elsewhere, finding a sense of belonging in my wonderful seaside environment, and also in school.

After kindergarten ended, my teacher said, "Frances, you've been a good girl. You're about to go into the first grade." I warmed to the favorable judgment, but when I thought about it, I wondered, *What does being a good girl have to do with it?*

On the first day of first grade, however, that compliment suddenly lost whatever luster it might've had. My new teacher, Miss Policoff, glared at me. "Frances Lief, you're *late!*" I slunk to my desk and cried. Drying my tears, I got a glimmer in my young mind that I would have to build my initial schoolgirl reputation anew. And I was well up to that.

<u>School was my safe haven.</u> Generally, I found my teachers to be fair, and I gravitated toward comfort with an ethnically diverse studentbody.

We moved when I started second grade, and I liked that school even more. For some reason, what sticks in my mind is the welcome feeling I got from the shiny, dark wood banisters on the stairways of my new school. The kids were friendly, and I settled into my new quiet passion for learning.

8

By the time I was eight, my eyesight had already begun failing. I wore glasses and didn't have the confidence to be as physically adventurous as my schoolmates. I never learned to skate, ride a bike, or enjoy a swing. So my energies flowed into academics, and I reveled being in school, where I felt that I belonged.

This affinity for education continued into high school. My enjoyment of academics balanced out to a large degree the vicissitudes caused by the Depression. It seemed that my family was effected by economic hard times more than most others we knew. In high school I wore hand-me-down clothes, which embarrassed me. I brought my own lunch and was never able to buy cafeteria food and enjoy it with all the other kids in the lunchroom. This hampered my social life. I had a few girlfriends, one or two of whom I would do things with after school. But these were limited friendships. Mostly, I retreated into intensive studying.

In four years of high school I only went to two or three parties, and I never went to the Friday afternoon dances. I was too shy, too frightened, and I didn't know how to talk to most kids my own age, especially boys.

I wrote for the high school newspaper, *The Chat*, and magazine, *The Dolphin,* and got an after school job at a local paper writing social tidbits at ten cents a news column inch. I belonged to lots of clubs in order to have them listed in the graduation issue of *The Dolphin.* But, in spite of my extracurricular activities there was little "stickum" between my classmates and me. I eluded popularity in a school setting, but fit in better with my contemporaries at the beach during summers.

I had one experience of being hurt at the end of my high school days that was of near-tragic adolescent proportions. My apprehension of not knowing how to dance was outweighed by the thrill of being asked to the senior prom. But I was stood up. When it became painfully apparent that my date would not be knocking at the door, I remained sitting dejected in the living room in my prom dress. Neither my mother nor my sisters-in-law offered any words of solace, just went on with whatever they were doing.

Although I had enjoyed elementary school and welcomed the academics of high school, I found college difficult. It was cold, impersonal, with huge classes. And, most important, no one imparted a nurturing spirit. Because of that, my inquisitive mind was blocked. I didn't understand the teachers, I didn't understand the textbooks. And I couldn't relate to the other young people. They were too proscribed and proper. Mine was a family of parlor pink socialists. I was brought up to consider the injustice of the case of Sacco and Vanzetti, and to respect the audacious writings of Heywood Broun. I had been raised to appreciate the radical columns of Franklin P. Adams in the *New York World*. Unlike most of my fellow college students, I cared about social inequities. To be out of step continued as a major theme for me.

I loved my home town all the more for my loneliness at home. The sights and smells and ocean breezes of my surroundings embraced me when my family didn't.

"Ten degrees warmer in the wintertime, ten degrees cooler during the summer." That's what the Rockaway Chamber of Commerce said to promote the sandy spit where I lived.

10

We were water babies. We knew the secrets of the beach, and how to keep from drowning as we tumbled in and out of the waves. The Atlantic Ocean is saltier than the Pacific. We could smell the salt and taste it. Here it is three quarters of a century later and I still am drawn to that delicious salty sweet air.

The Rockaway Peninsula is located on the south shore of Long Island in the borough of Queens, about an hour and a half from Manhattan by train. The peninsula is about ten miles long and a mile or so across at its broadest. On the south side of the spit was the boundless Atlantic. On the north was Jamaica Bay, a small inlet inserting itself between Brooklyn and the peninsula. There were good sandy bathing beaches, wide and narrow, running the whole length of the spit. No dunes. No rocks. No broken bottles. And no treasure, except for that of just being so lucky to live here.

Rockaway Beach was divided into a dozen or so hamlets. At the eastern end was Far Rockaway, adjacent to the mainland of Long Island. After Far Rockaway, going from east to west, came Wavecrest; Edgemeer; Arverne; Hammels; Holland; Seaside; Rockaway Park; Belle Harbor, where I lived; Neponsit; then the long stretch to Breezy Point at the western tip of the spit. There was Fort Tilden, with its hillocks and hidden bunkers of munitions. Many current residents wouldn't recognize the name Breezy Point, as it was changed to Riis Park around sixty years ago.

The history of the peninsula is reflected in the names of some of its communities. Mssrs. Holland, Hammel, and R. Vernum were all forward-looking real estate speculators in the late nineteenth century. Their personal holdings are long gone, but their names remain. Neponsit is an Indian name, and Rockaway itself is a corruption of Rockawackie, the Indian tribe who lived in what is now Brooklyn but summered on the peninsula to escape the heat of the mainland. There are remnants of Rockawackie graves on the peninsula, but the bones and skulls by now are duly packaged and labeled in the archives of the Museum of Natural History in New York City.

Living in Belle Harbor, my family was fairly close to the western end of the peninsula. My friends and I were the year-rounders, the winter kids. We knew the danger of the undertow; it was fierce, not to be ignored. We knew never to go swimming off Breezy Point where the ocean met the bay and the tides were mysterious, swirling, and forbidding. In Belle Harbor, sandbars would sometimes materialize a long swim out from shore. The brave kids would venture it, but not me. I wasn't that strong a swimmer.

On calm days, we'd dive through the breakers and pop up in the calm water beyond. One day when I was about twelve, I was diving through the waves when I found myself caught too far out. I extended my legs downward through the freezing water but couldn't find bottom. I was drifting toward Europe!

"Give me a hand!" I called out to the nearest bather, but either he didn't hear me, or didn't want to come out that far, so I kept drifting, desperately treading water. Suddenly I found myself in the firm grasp of a lifeguard, who tucked me under his arm and swam to shore. He plunked me down at the water's edge and walked away without saying a word.

I was mortified. I sat there on the shore with my head down, making believe I was playing with the

seems consistently
disappointed about people—
relies too much?

sand. No one came over to inquire, "Are you alright,
Frances?" I was utterly humiliated and sat silently for
a long while until I gathered the courage to walk back
up to the beach to my home. There I never said anything about the incident, believing nobody would really be concerned.

The population of Rockaway Beach in the 1920s
was a mix of blue-collar workers and white-collar pro-
fessionals, scholars, philosophers, thieves, and
scoundrels. I counted as philosophers the students and
working class people. I listed real estate speculators
among the thieves and scoundrels. For the most part,
the white-collar people were company middle man-
agers and shop owners. The blue collar folk were the
carpenters and plumbers who built houses, the
masons who laid down miles and miles of sidewalks
and driveways, and the garment workers who com-
muted between these oceanside communities and their
factory jobs in the city.

African American residents of the peninsula were
segregated to Hammels, which had deteriorated into
broken-down shacks that landlords didn't maintain.
The women hired themselves out as house cleaners.
The men were either maintenance workers or
employed by the Singer-Kelly Coal Company. Black
families from Harlem in the city had been enticed to
move out to Rockaway to take these jobs. House cleaning was thankless work, and shoveling coal from
barges to trucks to coal bins of steam-heated houses
was no better. These were dirty jobs at the bottom of why?
the economic ladder. I somehow identified with these
people, although my family wasn't as impoverished as
they were. We owned our own house.

13

Growing up as a lonely child in a middle class, comfortable home, I envied many of the black children. I was shocked by the poverty-ridden conditions in which they lived, but I so wanted the joyfulness and love they shared with one another.

The black neighborhood was eventually torn down and the residents removed to one of New York's first public housing projects, in an undesirable corner of Far Rockaway. The destruction of the community of Hammels was a disgrace, the placing of profit above people. The vacated land was turned into block after block of high rises, which further defaced the character of the area and the pristine natural geography of the ocean lapping against the shore.

Except for the Catholic kids who went off to the nearby parochial school, east enders and west enders got to know each other in Far Rockaway High School, as they still do to this day. The school was a blend of college-bound kids and those taking vocational courses. Among the graduates of Far Rockaway H.S. were Jonas Salk, discoverer of the polio vaccine, and Richard Feynman, who went on to win a Nobel Prize in physics as well as to share his heartfelt formulae for joyful living in non-scientific writings.

A common tie for the whole Rockaway Peninsula was *The Wave*, a modest weekly newspaper that covered politics, real estate offerings, and social events— power struggles, local and beyond; what was being bought and sold; who was born and who had died; and who was visiting whom. When I was sixteen I worked for a rival newspaper, *The Argus,* and shared all printable items of gossip with the young men who worked for *The Wave*.

14

Where we lived, 137th Street, was the first street to be paved on the four-block stretch from Jamaica Bay to the oceanfront (This was a typical item from *The Wave*). Little by little, sand disappeared from most of the roadways. My folks were willing to pay taxes for their own street to be paved, but not for any of the others. Politics prevailed, though, and finally the only sand to be seen was the strip along the ocean.

My parents moved to 137th Street in 1920. At that time, there were only a dozen houses from bay to beach, with sandy stretches between them. Most of the houses were two-story Dutch colonials with deep porches and dormered attics, built on standard size, 60x100 lots. There were hedges in front and sorry grass lawns that clung desperately to life.

We had a cold-water-only outdoor shower on the side of our house. My mother's daily diatribe was, "Don't come inside with sand on your feet!" Sand was bad for the plumbing and it scratched the hardwood floors.

Sand, sand, everywhere, and not a spot to grow anything but bushy silver maple trees and the wild sea grass that grew nearly two feet tall. It held the sand down and kept it from blowing all over the place. I loved chewing the tender, rootless ends of sea grass. It was the feel more than the taste that appealed to me. Sometimes I'd chew on it or make flutes out of it, and sometimes I'd braid it for the joy of its texture.

I loved the silver maples. One day when I was little, my father and I were walking to the beach when I saw a leaf shining silver in the sun way up at the top of a maple tree. "Papa," I said, "will you reach up and get me a leaf?" I wanted one because they were so shiny. But when he plucked one and put it in my hand I was disappointed. Taken down out of the sunlight the leaf wasn't shiny anymore.

From Rockaway Park up to Breezy Point, winter residents would share their private homes with summer renters. People have been coming to the Rockaway Peninsula for the past 300 years: first, the Indians, then the straggling settlers, finally the eager hordes of vacationers who rented bungalows and rooms during the summer. Rockaway's population grew steadily as New Yorkers recognized the benefits of the felicitous climate and the area's quietude.

In the 1920s, the summer people would arrive every year around the Fourth of July, crowding into the rickety bungalows and salt-worn Victorians of Edgemeer and Arverne. Often whole families squeezed into a single room. Some rented tents up in Seaside and camped along the wooden sidewalks.

For many year-round residents, renting rooms to summer vacationers was an economic necessity. We resented the summer people though we needed their largesse to pay our bills. My cousin Max characterized them as *lookniks, rentniks,* and *pascudniks,* the last of which is Russian for "impossible annoyances." With God's good graces, they were gone by Labor Day, leaving us to clean up their food shelves and medicine cabinets. We finally had our own homes just to ourselves again.

As the weather changed, we faced the problem of poor heating systems and large drafts. Mr. Krausse, proprietor of the Playland Amusement Park in Seaside, owned a number of houses that he rented to year-round people. He was a gruff, no-nonsense kind of fellow. Tenants would appeal to him, "Mr. Krausse, it's so freezing right now. Could we please have a bit more heat?"

"Why do you think they invented sweaters?" was Krausse's reply. End of conversation.

Our house was heated with pressurized steam, which in those days was fired with anthracite coal. You had to be careful with steam heat. "Watch the pressure," my father would say. "You don't want to blow up the house, do you?"

We were fighting not only the cold but also, after a few years, the Depression, and my folks could only afford to buy four or five tons of coal a season. In the winter, we just barely kept our water pipes from bursting.

Mr. Singer and Mr. Kelly owned the local coal company. It was an event when a coal truck drove up to the side of a house and sent the anthracite roaring down chutes into basement coal bins. Houses where we lived always had a winter sheen of coal dust, delicate and moist to the touch.

I was still raking the "clinkers," unburned bits of coal, out of the ashes when I was nearly forty-years-old. After the clinkers had been removed, the ashes were shoveled into cans and set out on the sidewalk to be emptied into the weekly garbage truck. Homeowners who could afford it converted to oil heat in the mid-1930s. It was a minor miracle. Later on, around 1950, when oil heat was abandoned in favor of gas, we were in ecstasy.

High school I recall as a time of innocent flirting. We lounged in packs at the beach, dashing into the water en masse, then running back up the sand to shake off the water and dry in the warm sun. Tanning lotions were unknown in those days, though I do remember some people using cocoa butter. I would drape a towel around myself to prevent sunburn. I didn't burn often, but when I did it was painful. The outer layer of peeling skin sloughed off when I took a shower. Winter kids knew better than to get sunburned very often, though. That was more of a problem for the summer folk, the seasonal invaders who took more sun than precaution.

In my pre-teen years, I used to visit my school chum Janet who lived down at the bay. I remember we used to play in her huge walk-in dollhouse. We would make clothes for the dolls and hide all the discarded cloth scraps underneath the dollhouse floor.

One day, instead of heading straight home from Janet's, I walked north toward Jamaica Bay. The road that ran along the north side of the spit was narrow and gravel-covered. We could climb down to the water's edge over treacherous rocks, but we hardly ever went down there because the water was usually so cold and the wind blew fiercely. But this day was warm, and as I walked down to the bay I saw a man fishing from the rocks. I watched as he pulled up his line, and there on the end was a wriggling eel. To my astonishment and revulsion, he skinned the eel alive! I turned away and ran home as fast as I could.

Our house was in the middle of the block. The wind blowing off Jamaica Bay was unforgiving and incessant, and the bedroom that faced north was abysmal. My folks used that room. My brother Harry's room faced south toward the ocean, and it was always warm and bright. It was the best and brightest room in the house. My room was next door to his, also facing south, but not quite as sunny as Harry's.

In the wintertime, my dad would go frost fishing with Mr. Wiedeman, the plumber; Mr. Waag, the electrician; other friends; and some of my brothers. They'd walk down to the beach at night in hip boots, carrying kettles and fishing nets. The kettles were left on the sand while the men waded out as far as they could into the breakers to scoop up the flounders that the tide had carried close to shore. They made great winter meals.

I enjoyed the lacy foam curling around the sand at low tide on sunny days. High tide could be calm much of the year, but in August it was rough, thunderous, unpredictable, totally schizophrenic. The breakers hit the sand in reckless anger, like as not bringing with them driftwood crashing up on shore. Those weren't good bathing days.

There was plenty of tar at high tide that would stick to our feet and on our bodies if we weren't careful. Walking on the beach wasn't so much fun on the very last summer days because of all the broken clam shells at that particular time. Eventually, though, the shells would sink into the sand or get washed back out to sea. We liked to gather the intact shells to decorate the walks around our houses. I used oils to paint seascapes in them.

Many years later, I was visiting Brighton Beach in England, and was surprised to find sharp rocks and shells underfoot as I waded out into the surf. It was downright painful to walk on them, yet this was a popular, crowded beach. The experience made me appreciate all the more my pristine local beaches.

I liked to go down to the beach early in the morning.

It was the gentlest time of the day. I could see the tracks of sandpipers and little bubbles in the sand where clams and crabs were burrowing. We rarely saw the creatures themselves, just their evidence in the bubbles.

We loved the seaweed with bulbous pods at their tips. When it dried, the little pods popped as we pinched them. Clamdiggers would make the most delicious chowder from their bounty. You had to be quick to catch clams. The seagulls picked them up in their beaks, then flew high into the air, dropped them onto the sidewalks, and swooped down to extract the meat in the broken shells.

Often we would walk down the block to the beach, barefoot with towels around our shoulders. It wasn't until about 1930 that an ordinance was passed forbidding people from being on the street wearing bathing suits with no robe or other outer garment. One day around that time, my brother Harry, who was an exceptionally young-looking twenty-seven, found himself on the brink of being arrested for having only a towel around his waist to cover his bathing suit.

"But I have to go to school tomorrow, " he protested.

"Well, I won't give you a ticket this time," the cop told him. "But don't let me catch you doing it again." The officer probably had no idea that Harry was a teacher, not a school kid.

My high school pal Marjorie lived a block over on 138th Street. Skinny dipping early in the morning was a special delight, and one day, by prearrangement, we took a dip at 6 A.M. We swam out to the farthest safety pole, where we jumped up and hung our bathing suits on top of it. We swam around until we felt like prunes. It wasn't until we were going to quit that we noticed a man on the beach watching us. We kept swimming, waiting for him to go away. He outlasted us, however, forcing us to jump up to retrieve our suits and expose our naked little bodies to his curious eyes. After we'd put our suits back on and began swimming toward shore, he went on his way, apparently satisfied.

Us winter kids, whether in grade school, high school, or college, would meet on the beach to dawdle the warm summer days away, flirting, swimming, and waiting for Joe the candyman to come around with his basket full of Crackerjacks, Necco Wafers, O'Henry bars, Snickers bars, and Mister Goodbars. Joe walked all the way from Seaside to Neponsit every day in his city shoes, dress shirt, and good trousers to earn his meager income.

These were the hard times of the Depression, but we always had a few cents to buy candy, and Joe's visit was the highlight of our day. We were sublime un-intellectuals, but out of our crowd ultimately came a couple of doctors, an inventor, a teacher, and a writer, as well as the requisite dedicated housewives and sincere but mousy husbands.

Summer weekends were busy days at the beach because of all the vacationers. Mondays, the beach-combers were at their busiest, raking up lost objects, including loose change if they were lucky. Once, a woman lost her wedding ring in the sand. Neither she nor her friends budged from the spot where it was lost until after sundown, but even though they fastidiously sifted the sand through their fingers for hours, the ring was never to be found. Or maybe later, some fortunate beachcomber accidentally turned it up.

A wooden boardwalk ran for seven miles along the ocean from Far Rockaway to Rockaway Park. There were stores along the way, benches to rest on, and couples would neck in safety and insanity under the boardwalk. On summer evenings, the boardwalk was always crowded, and the Fourth of July fireworks exploded in brilliant array over the ocean. Warm summer days stretched out long and lazy for schmoozing, reading, and swimming.

In spite of the summer interlopers renting our rooms, this was my season of greatest joy.

Getting Around—Getting Out

The decade between 1920 and 1930 was a peaceful time in Rockaway. New technologies were quietly coming onto the scene. Gaslight had disappeared from newly built houses, and oil was replacing coal in home furnaces. Telephones were starting to be used for social calls, not just for conducting business, and plug-in electricity was replacing batteries for radios. In 1927, "Lucky Lindy" made his non-stop flight across the Atlantic to Paris. It was the decade that saw the advent of sound in motion pictures, "talkies." The first one I remember was *The Jazz Singer*, starring Al Jolson.

It was the Roaring Twenties, the era of Prohibition and flappers with their unbuckled galoshes. Rockaway Beach became a favorite drop-off point for rum runners. Young men from Rockaway would row out to ships anchored in the dark and quietly and cautiously bring the bootleg "hootch" back to shore.

We would see ships out in the ocean on their way to Europe, and I wondered if my cousin Dick, who frequently had business abroad, might be aboard one of them.

A big part of living in Rockaway involved getting around the ten-mile spit. Our family did a lot of walking since the village was a mile away from our house. To get to elementary school I took a trolley car. To get to high school I rode a bus. To get to college I took the Long Island Railroad, as my cousins before me had done.

In my little community walking was a way of life. When my father picked that silvery leaf from the maple tree, we were taking a walk to visit the Noah Lief family who lived four blocks away. Uncle Noah's house was dark and musty, and Aunt Eva served stuffed dates, which I found bland and unpalatable. This was in contrast to the lively characters who lived there.

Of Uncle Noah's eight sons, five had married and moved away, but there were three bachelors still around, and they were energetic and full of fun. My cousin Max, dramatic editor of *The New York Daily News*, was constantly writing articles and books. He collaborated with his brother J.O. in writing song lyrics and scripts for Hollywood movies. Their one success in the latter category was a movie called *Two For Tonight*. The youngest brother, Alfred, was a quiet, industrious writer. To keep body and soul together he was editor of a trade journal. His best-known works were *The Dissenting Opinions of Mr. Justice Holmes* and *The Dissenting Opinions of Mr. Justice Brandeis*, but I especially enjoyed his biography of Lydia Pinkham, famous for her medicinals for genteel ladies.

My favorite was cousin Dick, who was attached to the Episcopal diocese of St. George's Church at Gramercy Park in Manhattan. He had exciting stories to tell of his trips to Russia and Africa. One day, Dick said to me, "Frances, you've changed. Now that you're a college girl, you've become a Lucy Stoner." I wouldn't admit to him that I didn't know who Lucy Stone

24

was. I later found out that she was a notoriously icon-oclastic thinker who retained her maiden name rather than take that of her husband.

In all, my extended family occupied six houses within the circumference of about a mile. My cousins and uncles took the Long Island Railroad to their places of employment, or to school in the city and back. The end of the line was 116th Street in Rockaway Park, the business hub of the west end, where they had their choice of getting the rest of the way home by bus, cab, or foot. Like as not, they walked, and they kept the local shoemaker busy in the process.

In those days, only two people in the family had automobiles: my father, with his Essex, and Uncle Oscar, who drove a Ford. I think Oscar paid $600 for his car. He and my father used their cars strictly for business purposes, not for pleasure. My Uncle Dillon, the most prosperous of all my uncles, bought a Cadillac, and my father set out to teach him how to drive. Shifting gears and steering at the same time proved completely unnerving to Uncle Dillon. He reached his limit when they ran into a dreadful traffic jam. Uncle Dillon broke out into a sweat, resolving, "I'll never touch a car again!" From then on he walked. No one seemed to know whatever happened to that Cadillac.

I rode the rickety-rackety trolley cars that ran a ten-mile route up and down the peninsula. I started riding them when I was six and kept on until I trans-ferred to a school that was closer to home when I was twelve. The pink trolley tickets used by elementary school children took us down to P.S. 43 on 110th Street, a mile and a half from my house.

On Saturdays, we would take the trolley down to the Park Theater to see the latest episode of *The Green Archer* serial that kids flocked to weekend after weekend. Once, to my surprise and dismay, the trolley conductor refused to honor my pink ticket. "That ticket is only good on school days," he said. "You can't use it on a weekend." Sadly, I got off the trolley. Seventy-five years later, I still wonder how The Green Archer rescued himself from the cliffhanger of that episode.

The trolleys all had motormen and conductors. The seats were caned with straw, two on either side of the aisle. The caning was impervious to the slings and arrows and assaults of exuberant kids. The trolley would screech to a halt, pick up a handful of travelers at my end of town, and clang on down the line.

The Green Bus Line replaced the trolleys sometime in the 1930s. It was a cooperative company, each driver owning a share of it. The bus cost a nickel, and we paid our fare as we got off. One time on my way home from school, I was about to get off, but as I reached out to put five pennies into the fare box, the driver stopped me. "No pennies," he snapped. All I had were pennies, so I hesitated. "No pennies," he repeated. I didn't say anything. Finally, I threw the pennies into his change box and ran from the bus as fast as I could. It turned out pennies registered as nickels in the fare box.

Once after school, Mr. Jones, my English teacher, gave several students, including me, a ride home from high school in his car. Since he lived even farther up into Belle Harbor than I did, I was happy for the ride. It was a pleasant drive, until just as I was getting out of the car I surprised even myself by turning to Mr. Jones and yelling, "You're stupid!"

"What did you say!?" he asked me in disbelief.

"You heard me!" I shouted, and ran off.

Whatever possessed me to do that I can only imagine. In contrast to my sophisticated cousins, Mr. Jones probably did seem stupid to me. Still, it was hardly a way to express my gratitude for the lift. But Mr. Jones managed to visit retribution on me. I got marks of ninety and above on all my New York State Regents exams, but only a seventy-nine on the English Regents—and that was my best subject!

what?

I mused about this to my high school chum Marjorie of those many years ago, and she said, "Of course, he marked you down. But you were telling him the truth, as no doubt his wife had already been telling him for years."

When I graduated from high school, I stopped taking the Green Bus Line, walking instead to the Long Island Railroad to get into Brooklyn, where I attended college. A group of us would meet daily on the 8:03. For most of the ride we busied ourselves doing homework or comparing class notes. The train would stop at Holland and Hammels before swinging around to Broad Channel, but when we left the peninsula and rolled over Jamaica Bay, everyone fell under the spell of the water's changing moods. The train made stops at Goose Creek, Hook Creek, an area called the Raunt, Aquaduct, and Howard Beach, before the end of the line at Atlantic Avenue in Brooklyn.

We walked from Atlantic Avenue to Brooklyn College on Court Street. Only when it rained did we take the subway; the nickel fare wasn't always easy to come by in those Depression days. When I did take the subway, I would often do so with my friend Max. I still

27

clearly recall the first time I had to walk down those steps by myself, with such trepidation for fear of what menace might be down there in the bowels of the earth.

One day, waiting on the subway platform with Max, the subway doors opened and I was confronted with a solid, steaming mass of humanity that had been crowded into the car like sardines. At first I froze, but Max muscled the both of us inside. I had never been in such close contact with so many strangers.

Back in Rockaway, walking was a way of life. Between our house in Belle Harbor and the commercial area in Rockaway Park, called the village, were twenty or so blocks of houses built around the turn of the century, interspersed among undeveloped sand-lots. En route to the village, we would walk past the beautiful wooden, black and white Catholic church, the beige stone Episcopalian church, and the modern brick synagogue. They were set among the newly constructed houses built in pseudo-Spanish style. For years, I walked the mile from 116th Street into the village early in the morning and late at night with no fear whatsoever.

My mother also walked back and forth along that stretch every day. She would do her marketing along 116th, sending home her orders from the pharmacy, the bakery, the butcher, the dairy, the florist, and the stationers, all of whom delivered their goods to customers' homes. There was a taxi stand near the Long Island Railroad station, and Harry Rayfield was the one and only taxi driver. Harry was a fixture; he'd been there seemingly forever. But my mother would never take a taxi or a bus to get home. Point of honor: she always walked. Maybe all that exercise accounts for why she lived to be ninety-eight.

Each one of our extended family's half a dozen houses held a special attraction for me. At Uncle Jake's and Aunt Molly's, I learned about Horatio Alger's rise from rags to riches. I listened in on endless conversations about the philosophy of Spinoza, and enjoyed the rowdiness of my three male cousins. They were pre-med students.

At Aunt Brina's and Uncle Louis's house, I loved the chandelier over the dining room table. It might have been Tiffany glass, for all I knew, and it dripped with what seemed like hundreds of strands of tiny beads. Just below the plate rails, which extended all the way around the dining room walls, were intricate stenciled designs.

Aunt Yetta and Uncle Dillon lived farther down the same block. I loved them and loved their house. The porch was deep and generous, and there was a cellar door to slide down into the back yard. The living room contained a Mason & Hammond grand piano, a harmonium, and inviting chairs and couches. Halfway up the stairs that led to the bedrooms there was another staircase leading down into the kitchen. To me, that was a magical passageway. The dining room walls were wood-paneled, and the windows looked out over the beach. Day and night, there was always someone eating in that dining room.

One day, I stopped into Uncle Dillon's house on my way home from high school and found my cousin Fritzi and her friend Lillian jumping all over the furniture. They were acting out Stravinski's *Rite of Spring*. The composer never had a more active or involved

29

audience than those two teenagers. I was too puzzled and shy to join in. Fritzi was six years older than I, was a music teacher, and gave me piano lessons from age eight all the way into the years of my marriage. I never learned to play with any facility, but she introduced me to Stravinski, Bartok, Chopin, Tchaikovsky, Sibelius, and several other composers who have enriched my life all through the years.

Fritzi was a wealthy man's daughter. Not only did she go to Juilliard, but she even had a car of her own to get to the houses of her music students. She was a brilliant pianist, a generous-hearted person, and a gifted teacher. It was from her that I learned the essence of teaching. One holiday, she staged a production of *Hansel and Gretel*. Fritzi and her husband were prompters, and each one of her students was involved. No one failed, and everyone—students, parents, friends—left happy.

Farther up the boulevard, was Uncle Oscar's house, clean and orderly to the point that it hardly had any life to it. At Uncle Noah's house, in contrast, the atmosphere was always spirited. But the most popular one of all was our house. My cousins enjoyed my mother's company, and they visited frequently. My mother could match them joke for joke, wisecrack for wisecrack, and she always had some kind of tasty goody for them.

There were a few skeletons in the family closet, but I can't talk about all of them since some skeletons are still rattling. One episode I can relate involved Uncle Oscar and Aunt Pauline. She was referred to by some members of the family as an unproductive cow. Pauline was always well-dressed and kept the house

[handwritten margin note: Why was she so unhappy there?]

30

clean and tidy. But she was otherwise lazy and, it seemed to most of us, also devoid of any sense of humor.

It was early 1928, in Aunt Yetta's and Uncle Dillon's dining room. I was twelve, and the only child around that day. I was in the living room, looking through books and magazines, because my mother and father didn't feel comfortable leaving me home alone.

My aunts and uncles around the table, ten in all, had convened at Yetta's and Dillon's house for a special Sunday afternoon confab. Conversation was carried on in a cacophonous but glorious mixture of English, Yiddish, and Russian. On the table was a basket of fruit, mostly apples, with knives for peeling, a bowl of nuts with nutcrackers and nut picks, sponge cake and honey cake, sliced lemons, raspberry jam, sugar cubes, and steaming glasses of Lipton's and Russian tea.

This afternoon was unusual I could sense because there was no light banter or joke telling. The collective mood was serious, without the normal laughter. At issue were the fortunes of Uncle Oscar and Aunt Pauline, the latter of whom had driven the former to near-desperation. What I heard was serious talk, set against Uncle Oscar's urgent, strident tones.

"I want to leave her!"

Low murmurs.

"I don't love her. I'm not happy with her!"

"Oh, Oscar. How can you say that?" asked Pauline.

"She's lazy. She never cooks."

"Oscar!"

"We're always eating out."

"Oscar…"

"She's selfish."

"Oscar!"

"When her niece died and left two little children, she didn't have it in her heart to take in these orphans and make a home for them" Oscar argued.

Murmur, murmur, murmur.

"I've got to get away from her. I'm not happy. There's nothing in that house for me."

Murmur, murmur, murmur.

"Oh, Oscar…"

"How will she get along?" Brina inquired.

"She has no money," said Yetta.

"You have a responsibility toward her," Jake interjected. "She can't be in the house alone."

No one spoke to the truth that Pauline was shiftless. They heaped the burden of the situation, and guilt, on Oscar. So Pauline stayed.

Sometime after that, overhearing a snatch of conversation between my parents, I found out that Oscar had a woman friend. I got to know her last name, and realized I knew her son because we went to high school together. Years later, Uncle Oscar's lover phoned my father, searching for Oscar. She hadn't heard from him in almost a week. Sad to say, Oscar had died.

Uncle Oscar "escaped" Aunt Pauline by having a fatal heart attack. And when I was twenty, I escaped my "*a*-social security" by venturing into the world on my own.

Not blending very well with the college crowd around me, in the mid 1930s I joined the Young

Communist League. I became a member because its stated philosophy of social equality matched mine. But even here I had a hard time conforming. The YCL's public activities didn't agree with my private nature. I felt uncomfortable trying to hawk *The Daily Worker*. I didn't care for distributing leaflets. And I abhorred making soapbox speeches.

I would have quit the YCL, except for someone who gave me incentive to stay involved. He was the only young man in all my life who had ever paid such serious attention to me. His name was Izzy Joe Neer. It wasn't long before we became sexually intimate.

My brother Harry had chastised me to conform to the standards of the household. Our mother had urged him to talk to me because I was having an affair with Joe. "Look," I said to Harry, "you're carrying on with your girlfriend, so what's wrong with me doing the same with Joe?" In those days, girls stayed "good" until they married—but not me. I was suddenly an emancipated coed, at least a generation ahead of my time.

My father said to me in private, "Don't marry Joe."

"Okay, I won't."

However, if my dear father had explained to me why I shouldn't have married Izzy Joe Neer, it might have made a difference. But he didn't—so I did.

Not right away, though. What I did do immediately was steal Harry's alarm clock (to get to my college classes on time), leave home, and move in with Joe. I spit in the eye of family disapproval and "lived in sin." What a shocking young girl was I!

seemed motivated by "shocking" family + not by love for Joe

33

Early Life with Joe

Joe and I set up housekeeping on Jerolemon Street in Brooklyn and after a couple of months, bending to social pressure, we got married. Sometimes his sister would stay with us for awhile; sometimes his kid brother would sleep over. We had a cute little apartment that Joe's mother had furnished for us. My friend Rena and I played young housewives, lounging over coffee while our husbands went off to work.

My exchange for these sunny days was that I had to tolerate my mother-in-law's contributions of food. If she wasn't the world's worst cook she had to have been a close second. She would bring a freshly killed chicken and flick the feathers all over the house before underroasting it. One morning, for breakfast I served to Joe and his brother the half-baked rice pudding she had brought over. They didn't want it. I said, "Joe, if you don't eat this pudding I won't let you go to work." Silence. They ate it. There was a barely premature irony in my nonsensical threat; Joe's problems with keeping jobs were soon to become evident.

Since I couldn't depend on him to make a living for both of us it was time for me to look for my own employment. My parents were getting up in years and I insisted that they go on home relief, making me eligible for a Work Progress Administration job. The WPA had been founded by the Roosevelt administration to help provide useful work during the Depression. Previous to living with Joe I was employed on a WPA project in Manhattan, typing and doing other office work. I made nineteen dollars a week as a clerk typist and, even though I was no longer living at home, I gave six of those dollars to my parents. Unfortunately, the project ended after a few months, and the WPA didn't have anything else for me.

I needed to find another job, and they were hard to come by. Once, I answered an ad in a paper for a file clerk, no experience necessary. I went to the place and like a fool said that I had experience. They didn't want me, so I told them that I had lied but they still didn't hire me.

At a second office, I interviewed, and they seemed hesitant about the job being available. I believed they rejected me because I was Jewish, so I said, "I'll prove to you that I'm not Jewish." I showed them my marriage certificate that was in the name of the Father, the Son, and the Holy Spirit. Ever since, I bear some shame for that cowardly falsehood. Luckily I didn't get the job, or the guilt would be worse.

Another time, a private employment agency that charged for job placement leads sent me into Manhattan's garment district. I had been advised to arrive for the interview early, so I did. I climbed the flight of stairs and knocked on the door. After a few seconds, it was opened by a yawning naked man with an erection. I promptly left, went back to the agency, and demanded my money back. They obliged me.

Those were but some of my sorry adventures trying to get work. Meanwhile, Joe was constantly being fired.

35

He was let go from a job my brother Mike found for him. Then, he got sacked from a furrier's job after two months; then fired from a plumber's union job after a couple of months. In each place of employment he insisted on telling his boss how to manage the business. Joe was always spouting left-wing politics, always out to change the system, and he wasn't an easy personality to endure, so he was continually being let go. Finally, he went down to Hammels and helped his father and mother run their dry goods department store. They didn't really need him working there, but they paid him enough so that he could at least buy food for us.

After I graduated from college, there was a moratorium on the city's teachers licensing exams. For the time being, my degree wasn't worth the paper it was printed on. I walked the Brooklyn Heights waterfront and found a job at the Harris Intertype Company, a manufacturer of linotype machines. My folks were puzzled by their college-educated daughter working as a factory hand, but the year and a half that I was there made more sense to me than the four years I spent in the Ivory Tower seclusion of books, lectures, and tests. At Intertype I learned to read blueprints, measure with micrometers and calipers, and spot-checked nuts and bolts as I read the greasy newspapers on my bench. Jolted into the blue-collar world, I soon learned that life was more than middle class, well-scrubbed America.

My bench mate chewed tobacco all day long, and spit the juice on the floor. I complained to the foreman until my partner was told to stop spitting.

I joined the International Association of Machinists

and went on strike, putting up with the angry glares and vicious, obscene slurs of anti-unionists. This was hardly any kind of life my family had envisioned for me.

I was only so rebellious, though. I had already succumbed to the social more of the day that a young, middle class woman should marry in her early twenties—older than that and you were dangerously close to being an old maid. Now I was to conform to convention by having my first baby, Billy, at age twenty-four. I gave birth to my second and last, Amy, five years later.

The employment officer begged me to stop working when my pregnancy began to show. I came out smelling like a rose, quitting as he wanted and getting severance pay. I used it to buy a Victrola and a good selection of records, including ones by Paul Robeson, Marion Anderson, and the Three Bs: Bach, Beethoven, and Brahms.

My mother urged me to return to Rockaway before the baby was born. With uncharacteristic wisdom, Joe said, "Let's not go." But, as usual, I didn't listen to him. *happens a lot* For once, that was a mistake. We went back to my childhood home, a sterile environment.

When baby Billy was born in 1939, I was stuck back in my mother's house, feeling deprived and as alone as I always had been there. I had a husband who would go to political meetings every night of the week, and parents who amused themselves with my baby. I was simply a vehicle for bathing, clothing, and feeding him.

I found myself constantly washing diapers, using my mother's old rolling pin to stir the boiling water.

After months of this, I was tired of it, feeling like one of Degas' weary, dispirited laundresses. I knew it would be easier if I bought a washing machine, the old wringer-type that was state-of-the-art then. This idea was ridiculous as far as my mother and mother-in-law were concerned. They both zeroed in critically.

"Why do you need a washing machine?" asked my mother.

"*I* never had one," chimed in my mother-in-law.

"I brought up six children washing diapers by hand," Mother added.

"Washing machines cost a lot of money," clucked my mother-in-law.

My mother tossed in the challenge, "How will you pay for it?"

"I'll buy it on the installment plan."

"You can't afford it," they chorused in unison.

It was easy for them to say; it was well past their diaper washing days. As far as I know, it was the first and last time those two women agreed on anything. Their double-teaming against me was to no avail. I bought the washer. My extravagances were limited, however. I had little money for extras, and even sewed my own dresses.

~

Billy was a marvelously smart little fellow. When he was two years old, I held him up to the window to see the snow coming down. He reached his tiny arms out and chortled, "Paper falling!" One afternoon, As I wheeled him down the street, Billy spotted the fire signal at the top of a telephone pole. "A orange!" he shouted, pointing at it. When Billy was three, he had an imaginary friend named Heinken. One day I asked Billy, "Where is Heinken?" He answered, "He's in Washington helping the government." Billy was a good-natured, amenable baby, but he cried every time I started to practice the piano. He knew at the sound of the first note that I wasn't going to be paying attention to him for awhile.

Waxing on as a proud mom, even though I was and still am, I have to admit that in my own eyes I was lacking as a parent in that I didn't have the natural inclination to be that affectionate with my own little kids, Bill and later Amy. Many first-time mothers have the cooperation of an interested husband or a compassionate mother. I had neither. How could I naturally take to hugging, kissing, playing with a child when I had never experienced these joys myself? These were songs my mother never sang to me, tales I never learned at her knee. My mother's modeling influenced my own limited demonstrativeness. This regret pains me still.

external control [handwritten marginalia]

Conforming as I did to the social acceptance of being a young wife and mother, I still was a misfit. I didn't make friends with the other young mothers around me who were busily comparing notes about the brilliance of their babies and exchanging recipes for formulas (this was in the days when breastfeeding was considered unfashionable).

I didn't have the money, clothes, or desire to be a "luncheon lady," and garden club meetings were anathema to me. I spent my early motherhood days feeding and caring for my little children, giving piano lessons, as well as taking them, learning to read scores by following recorded music. I had prepared to be a teacher, but was a professional without a job. And, in my own eyes, I wasn't even much of a mother.

Again, I moved out of my parent's home in Rockaway, when Billy was three. My mother and father had all the joys of playing with their grandson, and I had all the work and mundane responsibilities. We left, with no reference to Joe's opinion.

~

It became apparent within our first few years together that Joe and I were hardly the ideal couple; we were a mismatch. Out of my own naivete I had been swept off my feet by him. But I soon realized I'd better get back on my own two feet if we were going to maintain a roof over our heads. Joe's problem of keeping jobs only exacerbated my growing awareness of our being incompatible. Although Joe's family and mine were both Jewish, there were great chasms separating the Neers and the Liefs. The Neers clung to their ghetto roots. Joe's family and friends stuck to the old country habits while only tolerating New World customs. My family, on the other hand, gravitated to the American way of life and only kept a few European habits as incidentals of our tradition. Joe's family spoke Yiddish at home; my family spoke English. Joe's was a blue-collar background; mine was white-collar professional, even though I had experienced working class ways at Harris Intertype. It took me ten years to convince Joe to go back and finish his college education. In time, Joe suppressed his love of Yiddish song, dance, and humor that his

40

family so enjoyed. In retrospect, he would've been better off marrying a girl who shared his traditional customs and values.

～

My father died in 1944, when Billy was five and Amy was just two months old. My brother Harry offered me ownership of the family home if I would continue living there and take care of our mother. The last thing in the world that I wanted to do in my depressed and pressured state was go back to a situation that suffocated my spirit. I said to Harry, "Okay, I'll move back in the house if you put down new linoleum in the second floor kitchen and get the cellar door repaired."

He laughed—I left. I didn't realize it then but I was throwing away our family home. Sometimes you don't know what you're doing is right or wrong until you've moved down the road apiece.

～

By the time Amy was two years old, the New York City Board of Education opened up its teacher licensing examination after a ten-year hiatus. This was an opportunity that I had been waiting for since college graduation. I read books to study for whatever I'd be expected to know, and my friend Jean minded my children when I went to downtown Brooklyn to take the exam. I was well prepared and came in twenty-eighth out of 200.

When I started teaching, we sent Billy to a private school and left Amy in the care of a nanny, who was making more money than I was. But I knew that in time my salary would increase. Another way I eventually came to look at the situation was that the attention I should have paid to little Amy I was instead giving in my kindergarten class to other people's children.

In the spring of Amy's third year, I realized I could no longer remain living in the city. The leaves of the trees were turning green, and I wanted to again hear the foamy murmuring of the waves sliding up to shore and smell the scent of wild roses in the sea breeze. So, we returned to Rockaway, although not to my family's home, which by now had been sold.

Housing was scarce, and we finally settled for a tiny summer bungalow near the beach. We lived there for two years, getting through the winters with a wood stove for heat. The bungalow had two small rooms and a shower. Amy's bathtub was the kitchen sink.

One day, Joe came home and said, "There's a little house for sale a few blocks from here at Dashby Court. Abe Finkel told me about it. You should go take a look at it."

"Let's go together, " I suggested.

"No, you go yourself," he said. This was the kind of unilateral decision making that I was constantly dealing with. Joe would distance himself from most family matters.

In our ten years of marriage, from 1937 to 47, we had saved $1,000, which was what we needed to make the down payment on a $4,000 house. We bought the house, and borrowed extra money from the New York City Teachers Credit Union to renovate. Thus began another phase of our lives.

At Dashby Court: A House for All Reasons

Our family moved into the small house, which we remodeled and painted with an eye to restful color and comfort. It had three bedrooms, a bathroom downstairs, and a tiny sandlot of a back yard. Number Eight Dashby Court was in a cul-de-sac of a dozen houses that had been built by a Mr. Dashby in 1900. In 1950, the year we moved there, the houses were being renovated and each occupied by a family. The street in front was a safe playground for the children who lived in the court and their friends from more crowded adjoining areas.

We put in a long kitchen sink, and cut down the old wooden cabinets to half-size, using them as a kitchen divider. This gave us both a cooking area and a dining room. On the non-kitchen side of the divider we had an easy chair, bookshelves, and a work table for four-year-old Amy. Just an arm's reach beyond the kitchen window was a wash line on which I hung miles and miles of wet wash.

There was a tiny pantry for food storage, and a door leading into our miniature back yard with its canvas roof, comfortable beach chairs, and an entrance into the basement. It was good that we all were small people since the house was so compact. It was a replacement for the family home that we had so carelessly sold.

Number Eight Dashby Court indeed became a house for all reasons.

The Neer front door was a welcome entry to all and sundry. My niece Shirley and her husband Phil came out one summer with their year-old baby because they needed the reassurance that the sun and sand and sea and sky of Rockaway were still there in spite of the lost birthright of the family home in Belle Harbor. Bert, my brother Jack's son, and his wife Luisita, in their early days as starving art students at Cooper Union, were consumed with problems such as whether to buy two skinny sandwiches or one big fat one, but they always managed to scrape together the fare from Manhattan to Rockaway.

Our first year in Dashby Court was traumatic. I was exhausted from responsibilities, not only of housecleaning, cooking, and laundry, but also teaching during the day and going to college at night. There was simply not enough time to get everything done. I asked my mother to stay with us to help me. And in order to give myself a little surcease during the summer vacation when school was out, I invited my brother Mike and his wife Estelle to stay with us and keep my mother company. My idea was that my mother and her oldest daughter-in-law would keep themselves entertained so I could have some peace and rest. It didn't work out.

During this time, Mike, caring as he was, asked me, "Frances, what's the matter?" I couldn't answer him and just shook my head. I was terribly tired, and now stressed for another reason: Mike and Estelle had just blatantly taken over Dashby Court responsibilities. I was now a visitor in my own house. My mother and

Estelle, in effect, robbed me of ownership of my home, which depressed me. After awhile it got so bad Joe insisted that Mother, Mike, and Estelle leave. It took quite an argument to get them out. They seemed to think that my invitation for them to spend the summer was irrevocable, and I was roundly condemned by them for wanting the privacy of my own premises. But in anger and hard feelings they left. The summer passed, and I soon regained my self-esteem, working days and being a wife and mother at night. Joe, Bill, Amy, and I bonded in resettling the dignity of our lives, each pitching in to keep our little abode in tiptop order—without outside interference.

Another family intrusion happened a year or so later. One weekend, Joe and I planned to take the children camping overnight at Montauk Point. We needed someone to take care of Ma. She was over eighty by this time and had come back to live with us. I didn't want her to be alone, so my brother Jack agreed to spend the night while we were away. We started out for the point, with our tents, gear, and delicious picnic food. We were about to set our camp on the beach when a drenching rainstorm blew in. The tide was so rough and high that we would've been washed out to sea had we pitched our tents on the beach. We had no choice but to drive back home. We arrived in the middle of the night, and to my amazement, Jack got angry at us for coming home earlier than we said we would. In his mind, possession was obviously nine-tenths of the law. It's with amused retrospect that I look back on Jack's indignation.

Still, our door was always open for family visitors. When my bratty little nephew Jay came to spend a

45

week with us, he played stickball in the street with the other kids in the neighborhood and went swimming with them. His personality took on a sudden change for the better. He was happy and smiling. Alas, as soon as he saw his mother, who had come to take him back home, he reverted to his old whiny ways.

On weekends and holidays we would often travel upstate to our friends' farm near Cairo. Joe and I would pack up the two kids, our dog and cat, ten-pound loaves of pumpernickel and rye bread from the Star Bakery in Hammels, plenty of hot dogs and beans, and happily take off on the four-hour trip from Rockaway up to Green County on the western edge of the Catskills.

Bert and Luisita would frequently housesit for us. Our only caveat to them was that they watch the pressure gauge in setting coal-fueled steam heat in the house. We showed them how to start the fire, monitor the rising pressure, and how to bank the fire so the house wouldn't blow up. When we returned from our trip one time, Bert and Luisita were already gone. But the next time we were about to take off for Briskbrook Farm, Bert said, "What a hell of a time we had! We were either freezing cold or sweating like we were in the tropics. It's a wonder the house didn't blow up. And, as if that wasn't enough, you took the alarm clock! The only way we could make sure we'd get out of bed on time was to keep the radio on all night. We knew it was time to get up when we heard 'The Star Spangled Banner.'"

There were weekends when Fred, my brother Aaron's son, came out with his wife "Louise Number One" (he was to have two wives named Louise). Fred would go down to the beach and sketch the passing scene. One day, a woman he was drawing realized that she was his subject and began preening for his edification. But when she came over to take a peek at his art, her reaction was, "You son of a bitch!" That stylized picture, which Fred turned into an oil painting, hung in our house for years. I finally returned it to him, but sometime later changed my mind and asked for it back. He refused.

Recently, Fred, who we came to call "Racetrack Fred," brought up the subject of a painting of rhododendrons he had given me that I had hung in the bathroom. Fred asked me why I kept it there. "Because you didn't paint water in the vase," I explained. "The flowers needed the bathroom humidity."

When Fred and Louise visited us in Dashby Court, she would settle herself down in our back yard to write the Great American Novel. Louise never did finish her novel, but she enjoyed our good graces and returned the favor of our hospitality by bringing food to order. Whatever we wanted, or the children wanted, she would bring. There were bowls of macaroni and cheese, beef roasts, and huge portions of cherries jubilee. In those days, Fred was in the advertising game and made good money.

Sometimes I'd send picnic food down to the beach with the kids for whomever happened to be visiting: sandwiches, brownies, fruit, and whatever else had inspired me. Evenings in our cozy kitchen we would sit around into the wee small hours reconstructing the world in our image. The only sour notes to disrupt our harmony came from Joe and his political browbeating.

In many respects, these were good times for us.

47

Bill and Amy were doing well in school, and Joe had registered for a doctoral program at Columbia. We were both working and could pay our bills and enjoy small comforts. We agreed that Joe was working for bread and butter and I was working for dessert. Nevertheless, Joe's daily pontificating about his political beliefs wore me out. I was reluctant to ask my professional friends over to be subjected to his harangues.

When Joe spoke to people he simply didn't measure social situations, and like as not he was insulting. He would hammer everyone that his opinions were the only correct ones. I lived with a heavy heart that I could never develop lasting friendships with my school colleagues. Joe and I would be invited to people's homes once, but not again. He embarrassed me so.

Not thinking I could take it anymore, I called Fred once Saturday and told him that I was leaving home. I said that I'd packed my bags and Joe could take care of the kids until I found a place of my own.

"Don't make a move," Fred responded firmly. "Louise and I are coming out."

They made it there in half an hour, record time, to rescue me from myself. The two of them took me out to dinner that night and talked at me until I thought my head would burst. Then they took me back home. "You stay put," they said. "This is where you belong."

They reminded me of how my Uncle Oscar was pressured into staying with Pauline many years before. Fred would "rescue me" twice more from myself.

Many years later, I confronted him about the position he had taken. "Three times you coerced me to stay in that marriage, Fred. How could you?"

"Frances, if I knew then what I do now, after my own four marriages and three divorces, I would've let you do it." I suppose that was something approaching an apology.

—

Through those unhappy years with Joe, I also implored my mother for emotional support. "Ma, help me." All she did was wave her arm in silent dismissal.

Somehow consistent with her refusal to consider my desire to reject a man, my mother imparted to me how to attract one. By example she taught me how to flirt.

When she was in her nineties, living in a hotel for seniors, my mother was most likely still doing it herself. A fellow resident, drawn to her charms, proposed to her. She told him that she'd let him know the following morning.

The next day, he said, "Well, Mrs. Lief, will you marry me?"

"No," she answered. "My mother won't let me."

—

Amy was just starting elementary school around this time. She was a sweet-tempered child, with a cute face to match her disposition. The ribbons in her braids always matched her shoes and socks.

My daughter was a loving and beloved social butterfly, friends with all the kids on the block. They'd play on the cul-de-sac together. Amy was always ready with a box of cookies to share. She always ate with gusto, not like the other girls who picked at their food.

I was proud of Amy's resilience as a child, how she

accommodated herself to the vagaries of ill fortune. One day, she found out that she couldn't play anymore with Elizabeth, her best friend in Dashby Court, who was now going to parochial school. I assumed that Elizabeth had been told by her Catholic educators not to associate with Amy because she was Jewish. So Amy just walked down a few blocks to play with Sandy, with whom she attended the local public elementary school.

One afternoon, Amy was strangely quiet upstairs. I found her busily writing in her room.

"Mommy, my teacher said I have to write 'I will not talk in school' one hundred times."

"What!?" I said, infuriated. "Put that pencil down right now!"

I was in the school the next day, excoriating the teacher for punishing my child senselessly instead of merely explaining to her why she shouldn't talk in class. I gave Amy's teacher holy hell for that ridiculous assignment. Poor woman, I probably frightened her out of a year's growth. Later, Amy told me that her teacher had taken her in her lap and apologized. Then she said, "I love you, Amy. I hope you love me too." That touched me, and I encouraged Amy from then on to hush up in class.

My daughter never seemed to understand her own worth—nor did she share her feelings with me. How could I know why Amy was in anguish on the very Sunday the four of us were driving to the Museum of Modern Art in Manhattan? She'd promised Roger, who lived up the block, to marry him that same afternoon. What did she care about Jackson Pollock? I didn't pay enough attention to what Amy and her friend Sandy were talking about when they played dolls at our house day after day. I should have. Maybe I would have learned a thing or two about Amy's attitudes and her concerns about our familial relationships.

It wasn't until recently that Amy was finally able to relate to me about her misunderstanding of my stresses and strains during her childhood. She had read them as criticism of her. I've always loved her so much. If I could only have opened my heart enough to tell her that when she was growing up.

~

Bill was a practical child. He spent many hours in his grandparents' dry goods store eight blocks away, and many more converting our coal bin into a photographic darkroom. We put a sink in the basement for developing film and gave him money to buy what he needed for his new hobby. Bert and Luisita told Bill about the art and science of photography, what kind of camera to buy, and what other equipment he needed. Bill used their advice wisely.

During the McCarthy witch hunt years, when the FBI came to question me on suspicion of being a communist, as evidence they seized upon a photograph of an old man asleep in a chair. It so happened that the old man was black, and the FBI agents figured that my possession of the photo constituted left-wing sympathies. But it was simply one of Bill's better pictures.

Daily, Bill was down in the basement, working in his darkroom. He wouldn't be outside playing cowboys and Indians with the other boys. He was different. And to my way of thinking he was entitled to his individuality.

51

Eventually, Joe and I learned that Bill was gay, but when he was a child all we knew was that he was different.

In the summertime in our Dashby Court days, all the children went down to the beach together, as I had growing up when I lived nearby. They took their lunches and played happily at the beach all day, safe under the watchful eye of a lifeguard. As it had been with us years before, these winter children knew the way of the tides. It was still the visiting summer kids who usually got into trouble in the surf.

Our pets added much to our lives in the Dashby Court era. My brother Aaron asked if we would take his dog Dinkey for the summer. He originally had been my nephew Fred's dog. He left him with Aaron when Fred joined the Navy during World War II. The war was long over, but Aaron still had the dog, and was tired of walking it every night.

Aaron delivered Dinkey to us, along with his water and food dishes. Dinkey soon had the run of the street to pee wherever he pleased. Our animal kingdom already included our own dog, Mrs. Monte Woolley II; Birdy, an incessantly chattering parakeet; a cat named Worker, who insisted on eating at the table with us; numerous chickens; turtles; and a fish tank with stunning exotics. The addition of Dinkey was hardly an inconvenience.

Toward the end of summer, though, Dinkey disappeared. Bill and I ran up and down the boardwalk, up and down streets, up and down the beach, calling

"Dinkey..! Dinkey..! D-I-I-I-NKEY!" But we couldn't find him. We assumed that someone had stolen Dinkey, maybe mistaking him for Monte, also a wire-haired terrier, probably because they didn't like that we let our dogs run free.

There ensued the problem of calling Aaron to confess that we had lost his dog. When we fearfully broached the tragedy, though, Aaron exclaimed, "Thank you! That's the best thing that could've happened. Now I'm rid of that dog once and for all!" Years later, when Bill and I were reviewing past incidents, we concluded that Dinkey was probably walking home from the Bronx and got stopped at the Tri-borough Bridge toll booth because he didn't have the toll.

Worker the cat was quite a case. Not only did she put her paws on the table during dinner, expecting to be fed as if she were human, but she also regularly gave birth to litters of stillborn kittens. One morning, as we were rushing off to work, Bill found one of these litters in his closet and alerted us. "She's not through yet," Joe said. "You'll see. She's got another kitten in her." Sure enough, that afternoon when Bill and I came home from school, there was Worker, dragging a kitten behind her, still attached by the placenta. Monte was watching her also, and I grabbed her by the collar.

"Quick, Bill, sterilize the scissors!" I cried. "we'll have to cut the kitten free." But even as I said those words, Monte escaped my grasp, leapt over, and bit that placenta free herself. To me, it demonstrated a strong attachment between these two animals. Dog duty overcame cat abuse. Monty lived on to a ripe old age, a gentle, loving companion.

In 1955, when we moved to Bayswater, in the northern part of Far Rockaway, we found tenants for our little house on Dashby Court. This gave us a few extra dollars a month to help us pay the new mortgage. I only hope that the new family liked living there half as much as we did.

Getting My Professional Feet Wet

In 1944, When Amy was still a newborn, a friend and I started a nursery school in a tiny apartment just off Crotona Park in the Bronx. Nursery schools were a fairly new idea at the time, and they were in great demand because young fathers were still at war and mothers were working. I had the advantage of using my education as an early childhood teacher to set up a small facility, which was approved by the mayor's committee. That was tantamount to being licensed.

Our nursery school didn't last long, however. My friend and partner backed out after a year and a half. She wasn't cut out for this work, and I couldn't shoulder the load by myself, so we gave up our little enterprise.

At one point, that friend had advised me, "Joe's no good for you. You'd do better alone. If I were you, I'd get rid of him." But I didn't know how to do that and said as much.

I turned down what some termed "a golden opportunity" to teach at Parkchester, a school in an upper middle class neighborhood, to teach at a mostly African American primary school in the lower Bronx. I loved those children, who reminded me of the black kids from Hammels I had known growing up.

My enjoyment of being a teacher was in seeing how children would rise to levels of self-understanding if they were merely given enough time, encouragement, and sometimes space. I had established a buddy system in reading. Students would read in pairs. If one didn't know a word, his or her buddy often would. During reading time, Johnny G. once insisted on walking around the room while the others were peacefully in their seats. Knowing that he was a troubled child, neglected at home, I just let him do it until he got it out of his system. After this defiant behavior had gone on for a few minutes, his reading buddy looked up at me with irritation.

"Mrs. Neer, why do you let Johnny walk around when the rest of us are sitting down?"

"That's as far as he can go," I responded.

Maybe realizing that I wasn't going to give in to his need for attention, Johnny sat down.

One time, I asked each of my students, "What was good for you since you came to school?" and each answered into a tape recorder. "I learned to make friends," "I learned to read," "I liked when my mother came to school," etc. Then I asked Johnny G., "What about you?"

"I learned to read." Then, sheepishly, " I learned to shape up."

Encouraging his need for self-expression, I said, "Is there anything you want to add?"

"Yeah... shit!"

With teaching, came the rewards of being with kids' wonderous imaginations. One of my first graders asked, "What's on the other side of zero?" He had a concept of negative numbers!

There were also the payoffs of long term investments in kids who had to work a little harder. Reading, being frozen speech without inflection, was difficult for some of my students. There was one child who had a particularly hard time learning to read. I didn't push it. Finally, one day he looked up from his book, beaming, and said, "I got it!" We were both on Cloud Nine.

Even with so-called "problem kids," by letting them alone, just offering material to them, I discovered that they usually would find their way. Once I read an article in the *New York Times* about turtles, then prompted my students to write about turtles. At the end of the school year, each child had written their own turtle book.

My hands-off encouragement rather than traditional hard line instruction seemed contrary to most of the rest of the faculty. But the "bad cases" were often dumped on me. I suppose my attitude about teaching was based on my own childhood. I liked teaching first *her golden age* grade—kids who were six years old. It was at the age of six that I came to feel intruded upon in my own home, disregarded. So, I gave my students relatively free rein out of respect and the deepest regard.

What also regretably stays with me are the mistakes I made when I first started teaching. One of the first grade mothers came to me with her concern that her son was writing backward. Not knowing what to do about the problem, I just minimized it by giving her the glib and ignorant assurance, "He'll grow out of it." Little was known then about learning disabilities or how to treat them. But there was still no excuse for my irresponsible stupidity.

At another time, years later at another school, I misused the perception some parents have of a teacher being omniscient. A mother came to me distraught that her son wouldn't eat eggs. What the hell was I supposed to know about dietary stimulation? Not seeing any real problem (let him have cereal instead) and probably being in a frivolous mood, I recommended that she make a pinhole in an eggshell and encourage her son to suck the raw egg through the hole. Well, the boy really took to that, sucking out four or five eggs to a sitting. If he ever had problems with high chloresterol (something else we didn't know that much about then) I'd have to bear some of the blame.

There's such a pleasant memory I have of my fellow teacher, Clara Kramer, and I putting on an Easter show for the school with our classes. We taught songs to our kids, made festive hats with them, and Clara played the piano to accompany their singing for the show. Our school principal was quite impressed, saying that there never had been such an elaborate musical review at the school. He only regretted that we didn't tell him beforehand how much of a production we were staging or he would've brought a camera.

When I had a look at the IQ tests that were given to my little first graders, I realized that the tests were unfair and invalid. These poor kids, for instance, didn't know the word "porch." The humble houses they lived in didn't have porches. I may have been ignorant about learning disabilities, but even back then I had some awareness of cultural bias in school testing.

Forward thinking was also with me when I established parent/teacher conferences throughout the school year having to do with how children were getting along, not necessarily about their having any kinds of problems. I believed that they would help parents get more involved in their children's education. From conferences throughout the school year, parents would become more supportive of their kids' learning processes.

With my own husband, though, I did something that I'd never encourage with the parents of my students. I happened to visit one of Joe's college classes, and his teacher told me what a good paper he had written. Little did she know that I was the one who had written it.

Thank You, Joe McCarthy, You Bastard!

It came to pass in 1954, that Joe Neer's big mouth, in defiant opposition to the overwrought anti-communist zeitgeist of the day, was going to get me fired from teaching. It was inevitable. I was seen as guilty by association. The best I could do in the situation was to somehow get disability retirement. I conferred with Abe Letterman, then president of the teachers' union, who asked me, "What kind of disability do you have?"

I didn't know.

Soon thereafter, I complained to my doctor about being more tired than I thought my job and family responsibilities warranted.

He said, "You probably have a chemical imbalance, Frances." That was the key to my getting what I wanted, though I still needed a convincing way to communicate my "need" to the powers that were. Don't try to engage them, I wisely thought. Just stymie the hell out of them.

As sort of a rehearsal, in effect, I was questioned by an attorney for the Board of Education. He asked me if I knew any of the people in our neighborhood who had signed a recent petition endorsing left-wing issues. Although my husband, naturally, was one of the signers, I gave the attorney nothing substantial to consider about me. I simply said, mostly as non-sequitor, "Rockaway is ten miles long," and he questioned me no further.

The teacher's union referred me to a therapist who had experience dealing with the confounding ways of the board. He told me that when I went in for my physicians' eligibility review (a rubber stamp process before retiring anyone) there would be a secretary chatting to a friend of hers, who would seemingly be involved in her knitting or whatever. But both of them would be observing me closely, so I shouldn't say a word. Good advice, I'm sure. I kept mum until summoned into the room where the review board was convened.

One doctor asked me if I made lists when I went marketing. I assumed this was a trick question to somehow incriminate me.

On impulse, I merely responded with a quietly tortured sounding, "My son, my son..."

Another doctor asked if my husband was dead.

As if oblivious to what he had asked, I just repeated, "My son, my son..."

After a few more questions, all being met with my same response, the head doctor said to his colleagues, "This woman belongs in a hospital." That ended the interview.

Bingo! I was going to get my disability.

Saving my job was impossible. If I really thought that there was any hope of that I probably would have been crazy. But on pure instinct, in acting crazy—like a fox—I had salvaged some recompense.

Teaching I had always loved (and still wasn't

61

through doing), but not being answerable to the Board of Ed. Bureaucracies and me have never been a good mix. So I owed thanks to two Joes: my husband, for being so vociferous about his politics that he brought unfavorable attention to me, and Wisconsin Senator Joe McCarthy, with his toxic, infectious paranoia. It was a dark time, but for me this cloud had a silver lining.

did she still prescribe to her earlier communist Idealogues?

Is she visually impaired?

Independent and Involved

By 1956, I had had a variety of jobs, easily come by with my background in child development. I enrolled in graduate school at New York University. We had bought the new house in Bayswater, away from the blue-collar community of Dashby Court. Bill and Amy were now living in a safe, middle-class neighborhood, especially appealing to Amy. Joe was working in his parents' store.

And I took a lover.

While still teaching in an elementary school a few years before, I had met a man named Jay when he came to my classroom on Parents' Night. It so happened that he was the father of the egg-hating kindergarten kid whose mother I had glibly advised to have her son suck raw eggs through pinholes in the shells. I had known Jay's younger brother Teddie years before. He had married my cousin. Teddie stood out in my memory as having been kind to me when I was a child, so it was easy to transfer my love for Teddie to Jay.

Jay and his family lived across the street from where we now lived. It took seemingly no time at all for him to make advances toward me, and no time at all for me to reciprocate. Our four-year affair was conducted clandestinely. No one noticed when Jay would come over to our house to pick up the bridge column from the *New York Times*. When he'd be casually singing, "Let me call you sweetheart," I knew who he meant. I would sometimes call him at work to confirm a date. Occasionally, his business partner would answer the phone and tell Jay, "Here's the woman with the lovely voice wanting to talk to you." Once at a party over martinis, Jay's partner heard me in discussion with someone. He turned to me without speaking and his eyes said it all. *Now I know who Jay's enamorata is.* That moment cemented my fondness for martinis.

Both Jay and I felt desperate in our frustrating marriages, and we sought relief in each other. I learned then that true love is expressed in giving without expectation or need of anything in return. In fact, giving love can even be synonymous with getting it.

When his wife died, Jay moved to California and, coincidentally, we bought my in-laws' house in Woodmere. So Jay and I each left that middle-class community that had been so comfortable for both of our families. Unfair to Amy as it was, we uprooted her from her high school and moved.

Years later, Jay's son phoned me. "Frances, this is Rick. Dad died."

"Oh, Rick, I loved your father."

"Yeah. We kids always knew it."

———

At the beginning of the '60s, I spent four years as a first grade teacher at an independent school, Woodmere Academy, then moved on to more fertile fields, thanks to President Johnson's War on Poverty.

I became director of community education in a

program sponsored by the University Settlement House in New York's Lower East Side. Here I developed a homework assistance program in which college students would help poverty-stricken Puerto Rican children with their homework.

A particularly sensitive client group was illiterate men. I admired them for pushing through the shame they felt to improve themselves. And I also realized that we were in competition with that shame, so we'd better get results fast for these men to stay with the program long enough to become literate. It seemed to me the best way to do that was to make learning to read of immediate relevance to these men. Most of them either worked in a nearby garage or were interested in cars, so our reading texts were auto repair manuals. Another educational priority was having the men learn to read menus and names of subway stops to help them overcome their embarrassment in dating.

But the star program I spearheaded during that time was the *La Cooperativa de Madres,* a childcare co-op by, for, and of Puerto Rican mothers. Social workers who had these women on their caseloads didn't understand why I wasn't working with them in the standard ways of service delivery, "by the book." Thinking that I probably wouldn't find out about how to work meaningfully with those of another culture from books, I spent time in the clients' neighborhoods to learn first-hand their needs.

The *cooperativa* wasn't essentially my idea, although I give myself credit for just being open to listen. Inquiring of these young mothers about their lives back in Puerto Rico, I found out that as families they had lived cooperatively in their villages in helping each other build houses. So why reinvent the wheel? Just adapt the same spirit to mutual child care. The *cooperativa* was anything but a new concept to teach them and hope they'd buy into. I came to realize that the field of social work would be much better served with less theorizing and more common sense.

The *cooperativa* was in a one-room facility that could accommodate eleven children, from birth to four years old. We had cribs, little tables and chairs, books, toys, and all the equipment any good nursery school would have. This was acquired through personal donations, most of them from my friends at Woodmere Academy.

The parents' support was given not in money, but in time. That was the payback: time to share and time to learn. A mother made an appointment a day or two ahead to bring in her children and said how long they needed to be there. Then on another day, that mother would come in to help with other children for a similar amount of time. The children benefited, and the young mothers learned about different ways of child care.

Although I had started the *cooperativa*, I didn't work there. I was the wrong age and color. I hired a Portuguese nurse who looked Puerto Rican. She also looked the part because she always wore a white uniform. One morning, I found out there had been a fire in the neighborhood the night before and the *cooperativa* facility had been converted to a dormitory shelter. I've always felt good about this integration with the community, and that neighborhood residents considered it a safe haven they could use in an emergency.

As far as I know, *La Cooperativa de Madres* still

exists. When it began it was, in essence, a pre-Head Start program. These days, of course, child care centers for newborns to pre-schoolers are commonplace.

I stayed with the community education program at the University Settlement House for a little more than a year. Having accomplished pretty much what I wanted, I moved on to a new and much different challenge, taking a position instructing at a women's teachers college in the town of Willimantic in eastern Connecticut.

It was not so far from where I grew up, geographically, that is. But what a different world I found myself in! So Yankee, so off-the-Mayflower traditional—so lily white. I passed through communities whose signs proudly proclaimed, "Founded in 1802," "Founded in 1746," Founded in 1668." It seemed less of a place than an institution, and the senior students I had reflected this attitude. They all came from rural areas outside of Hartford, all were the first in their families to go to college, and all were firmly immersed in the status quo. They had been trained to mimic whatever their teacher said. I found no real flattery in that and didn't want it to be the case with me.

Frank, a social worker I knew, came to class one day and I urged the young women to speak up, tell him what was on their minds. A vacuum of silence. My students just looked at each other in mild bewilderment.

I turned to Frank and said, "Look at these future teachers. They won't even tell you their educational concerns." I couldn't help but tip my political hand. "I'm trying to turn them into Democrats and they insist on remaining Republicans."

In time, though, these young women came to trust

me. I only hope that my influence helped loosen up some of their conservative thinking.

I took a year's sabbatical, went up the road apiece, and enrolled in doctoral courses at the University of Connecticut in Storrs.

At the end of that school year, we gave up our sweet little house in Willimantic and returned to New York.

PART 2

WEST COAST—
NEW NAMES, NEW GAMES

Taking Horace Greeley's—and Bill's—Advice

We lived in Manhattan. We spent five interesting years in a high-rise on Worth Street, a couple of blocks from city hall, at the edge of Chinatown. For the time we were there we ate our way through the food of every province of mainland China. We left just as we were beginning to eat our way through the Italian cuisine of Mulberry Street. I was an assistant professor in the city university system. Joe sold what had been his parents' dry goods business and became an elementary school teacher. Those were good days for him, teaching fifth grade, ten-year-old Chinese children. He did very well with the kids. He respected them and they respected him. He related well to his students, but, in his usual contentious way, antagonized the school's administration. What else was new?

another negative description of Joe

After earning his Ph.D. in psychology, Bill moved to San Francisco at the urging of a friend and graduate school colleague. He had told Bill that California was ripe for therapists and he would find it easy to establish a private practice there. But Bill was no longer interested in being a psychologist. He wanted to use what he'd learned in grad school about human thought and behavior to his advantage in business. So, off to San Francisco he went, hoping to buy up the City, parcel by parcel. Over a few years, Bill became quite successful.

In 1974, I got a series of phone calls from him, concerned about his father's insane way of acting. Bill said, "You cannot treat irrationality in a rational way."

"Yes, I know," I answered. "What can we do about it?"

There was a pause on the other end of the line, then, "We'll think about it."

Bill called again the following week. "Why don't you guys retire?"

"We'll think about it," I responded.

Bill called a third time. "Send money. I bought you a house."

The next call was from me to Bill. "We're on our way. The mover's packing us up and we'll be out in a week."

Journalist Horace Greeley had said, "Go West, young man!" And Bill had said, "*Come* West, Mom and Dad! Come to San Francisco."

I was ready for a change in scenery, and Joe went along with the idea of moving. Bill had married, and he and his wife Ann had a little girl, Christine. There was new family to add to the attraction of relocating.

One of the first things we did upon arriving in San Francisco was buy an opera subscription (We'd had a Metropolitan Opera subscription for many years). Then we had Joe start working as a bookkeeper for Bill. He had bought a restaurant, The Sausage Factory on Castro Street, and learned what ingredients were needed to make good pizza. At one point, Bill was buying more cheese than any other restaurant owner in the City. He managed the menu, the kitchen staff, and waiters. And Joe took care of the receipts. In short order, of course, Joe was *the* expert in the restaurant business, telling Bill in front of anyone how to run things. The father, who'd been given a job by his son, proved to be an increasing embarrassment.

As for myself, I managed to do nothing but learn how to crochet. Then the City College of San Francisco phoned to ask if I was interested in a job. They needed someone to develop a child care center for students who were parents. I took the position, but again found myself pretty much alone in a crowd. I made friends with a few people at City College, but was more comfortable spending my time learning the art and craft of doing stained glass. The people I met in San Francisco seemed to be totally imbued with the '60s revolution. Although I was sympathetic to many of their causes, I was older, and felt like a conservative New Yorker by comparison. I gave up my job at City College because I didn't fit in with the people I was working with, and didn't feel that they understood me.

At the same time, I registered for a gerontology certificate at San Francisco State University, and got a second masters degree in low vision studies at City College. Finally, I started making some new acquaintances.

Joe and I had left longtime friends on the East Coast who'd grown to tolerate Joe and his cantankerous ways. In San Francisco he found new friends at the public tennis court where he played. But they were mostly young singles and these associations didn't last long. New opera subscription or not, the move west shook up Joe's and my marriage within a couple of years.

After one of our characteristic disagreements one day, I looked my husband in the eye and said, "Please leave. I can no longer abide you." And Joe left without

73

objection, as if he too realized that we had never really had been good for each other.

Not that we didn't have some nice times, and we shared our love and concerns for Bill and Amy and later Christine, but I'd known almost from the beginning that life with Joe was harder than it had to be, certainly more so than I deserved. I was also convinced that it was never going to get any easier. Why had I stayed with him for thirty-nine years? As a child I had grown up alone in a crowd. I remained so long with Joe because I was afraid to be alone again. This feeling hadn't left me. I'd just gotten to the point that I was more lonely with Joe than I might be without him.

I continued doing stained glass, finding it was just what I needed. There was art in cutting the glass in my own designs, and craft in leading the pieces together. One design turned out to represent essences of my life. I had put small mirrors in it, reflecting who I was; thin shards of glass, spokes radiating out to show my spirit of outreach; and waves and spikes, indicating quality of direction of my actions. I didn't realize the graphic symbolism of what I had done until the work was completed. The owner of the glass shop where I bought my materials liked the piece enough to display it in her window. This was vindication of sorts for my first stained glass effort that Joe had pooh-poohed.

The move to the West Coast was the straw that broke the camel's back of my marriage. This quiet upheaval freed me to discover more facets of myself, new ways of looking at who I was now and perhaps always had been.

74

But after Joe left, I realized that I was used to having a man in the house. "Mom, you're a risk taker," Bill said. "Put an ad in *The Bay Guardian*. See who turns up."

So I did. Would the years with Joe prepare me for new experiences with other men?

Ever the Twain Shall Meet: Frances Lief Neer and Jeremiah Franklin Becker, Jr.

My ad was simple and forthright. It said: "Retired professional woman, 62 years young, would like the companionship of a gentleman in similar circumstances." Out of the five replies, I discarded the first one that had been written by an educationally challenged person. I rejected the second from a man who was clearly still recovering from a divorce and a trip around the world that had failed to heal his sadness. Obviously, we had too divergent reactions to the end of our marriages. I threw out a third response from a man who was willing to rent a car so that I could drive us around. I hope he found a good chauffeur. I discarded a fourth letter from an overly needy fellow who had written five pages promising me the sun, the moon, and the stars. He was so anxious that he had included a self-addressed, stamped envelope. When I told one of my friends about this letter, she said, "Oh, did you go out with him?" "No," I said. "I threw the letter away and kept the uncanceled stamp."

The fifth response to my ad I found provocative and challenging. The letter had been written in February on Christmas stationery. The handwriting had old-fashioned curlicues. Out of the envelope fell a snapshot of an elderly gentleman in western attire:

76

cowboy boots, string tie, and chaps. He was holding at his sides two little boys. At his feet was a border collie (whom I later got to know as Sandy, the smartest little dog in the West). In the photo's background was a fence, upon which rested an enormous wheel from a Conestoga wagon. The cowboy's name was Jere Becker, and going out with him would be about as far away from New York as I'd ever ventured.

But I didn't go anywhere just yet. Jere and I corresponded and only spoke on the phone for a couple of months; he wouldn't come to San Francisco. He hadn't driven to the City for several years, and didn't want to spoil his record, I guess. I, in turn, wasn't willing to travel to his ranch 100 miles away. It was a stand-off. Then one day in April, my new pal of few words and sly humor sent me a clipping from his local newspaper. It was a photograph of two teenage girls on horseback. The headline read: "The Best Rodeo in the West." Thus, Jere Becker gambled on my curiosity and figured that I needed to experience something of his way of life. I didn't know anything about ranches and rodeos. So he was right; I had to go and find out.

As we rode from the Modesto Greyhound station to his ranch, Jere kiddingly said, "I'll give you forty-nine per cent of what I own."

"Uh-uh, Jere. That won't do. Divide it up fifty-fifty."

I thought that this man was so in need of a new relationship that he'd be willing to play along. But as decent a man as Jere turned out to be, he was also a skinflint.

In all fairness, Jere was a hard working rancher. His money came from the sale of beef cattle and sheep.

Most of his available cash was used to pay taxes and debts to bankers for loans to maintain his ranch. One of Jere's common expressions was that the winter weather "was as cold as a banker's heart."

We drove from Modesto twelve miles to his ranch in Oakdale. As we rode onto his property, this naïve New Yorker saw before her a landscape that appeared to be a cross between the opening scene in *Oklahoma* and a stage set from *Tobacco Road*. On either side of the rutted road were scraggly almond trees. There were a couple of broken-down cars in front of the barn. Cattle and sheep were grazing wherever I looked.

Coming into Jere's house through the back door, his kitchen was a shocking sight to this orderly housewife. It was a great modern kitchen with picture windows on either side overlooking acres of pasturelands, so that the outside, in effect, was also inside. But there was a huge marble table covered to overflowing with newspapers. It was a mess. Jere had been batching it since his wife died three years before. As I looked more closely, however, those papers were all *Wall Street Journals*. I forgave Jere's sloppiness on the spot. The contrast was just too captivating.

It so happened that he was a graduate of Pomona College, attended the University of Mexico on a scholarship, and had been enrolled in the School of Economics at Harvard. He was a voracious reader and had a remarkably retentive memory, with a keen grasp of history, geology, and anthropology. There was more to this "hick" rancher than at first appeared.

My first day on the ranch turned out to be interesting and provocative. Jere excused himself. "I need to switch the irrigation valves in the pastures." He had already shown me the bedroom that I would have for my own, and pointed out the crowbar I could use to lock the door from inside. That day, his bedroom was neat and tidy, probably the only time in all the years I knew him that he ever made his bed. But it had a rise running down the middle of it that made the bed look like a pup tent.

"What's that?" I asked Jere when he returned.

"A bundling board. That's what kept a young couple cozy and not too close in the cold days of yesteryear."

I thought about his messy house, the newspapers piled up on the kitchen table, his ashtrays overflowing with cigarette butts—and that ridiculous bundling board.

When he was about to sit back down with his wine, I said, "Jere, get that goddamn board out of your goddamn bed." He did so promptly, without saying a word. And as he took the board through the living room toward the back porch he had a smirk on his face like the cat that ate the canary.

That's when our relationship got rolling.

Soon after returning home from my first time at Jere's ranch, my friend Robert from Bloomington, Indiana traveled out to spend some time with his sisters in Berkeley. They all drove over to visit me. As Robert stepped over my threshold, he said, "Frances, marry me."

"No siree, bob, Rob. You'd nag the hell out of me." Robert thought he heard wedding bells. Now that I had met Jere, though, I heard cow bells.

Jere and I were quite a contrasting pair. I never imagined that I would have lasted nearly a decade with a western rancher—and a Republican, yet! Jere defined me as "an easterner with willful ways." And he would tell those we met, "Frances is a do-gooder." But we were complementary in our backgrounds and natures. Also in our senses: I was starting to lose my sight, and Jere was becoming hard of hearing.

In the close to ten years we were together, Jere and I divided our time between my flat in San Francisco and his ranch near Oakdale. Sometimes we'd spend a week or two in the City. Other times I'd stay a couple of weeks out at the ranch. We did a lot of driving through California, north to Oregon, and down into the southwest in Jere's camper. We would spend a month or two each year out of the country, and in nine years we circled the waist of the world.

Bill often drove out to Oakdale with Christine on weekends. He would smile at me and say, "From a New York sophisticate, you've become a ranch wife."

Jere and I knew we wouldn't marry. Neither of us felt any need to do that, perhaps heeding the wisdom of Dr. Samuel Johnson, "A second marriage is a triumph of hope over experience." The term "significant other" had not come into the culture, nor had the word "partner" in reference to unmarried couples. To call ourselves lovers was overly romantic for our acerbic way of relating, so we simply introduced each other as "my friend." When I introduced Jere to people in San Francisco I would often say, "This is my friend Jere. He knows everything, and I know the rest."

As a man of the earth, Jere's philosophy was quite simple: Let two blades of grass grow where only one has grown before. He was a natural environmentalist, an organic rancher who didn't use chemicals.

80

The food we ate was as pure and fresh as the air we breathed. I learned to make the best Swedish venison roasts this side of Delmonico's in Manhattan. Tomato sauce for spaghetti was made from scratch. One weekend, our company loved that spaghetti so much that I made three pots of it. We would barter calf's liver for a neighbor's corn or asparagus. This was all so different for me—and marvelously pleasant. I enjoyed happy relaxation and the energy to embrace a new way of life.

One thing, though, I soon found out not to make light of. When Jere's rancher friends were visiting I heard their seemingly endless discussions about water. *What's the big deal*, I thought. *Turn on the faucet and you get water. Why do they go on about it so?* I soon learned the meaning of drought, and that Jere's well was supplying water to several of his neighbors whose wells had gone dry. Back on the East Coast, we'd taken water completely for granted.

My New York accent differentiated me from Jere's other friends, probably putting them off. And it was hard for some of them to understand. When we first knew each other, Jere and I would commonly respond to whatever the other had said with, "What did you say?" "Huh..?" His western plus Harvard dialect and my New York inflections were mutual unfamiliars.

At the ranch, I came to revel in the country sounds of the night. I loved the hoot of the owls, the clicking of the crickets, the low mooing of Jere's cattle, and the stamping and whinnying of his horses.

One day, I had dressed up all in white, looking as if I was going to play tennis, when Jere said, "Frances, I need you to help me move the cattle into the corral.

Stand right here across the opening to the barn and hold these branches in both hands to keep these dogies moving straight along. Don't let them get diverted into the barn." Sandy, Jere's little border collie, nipped at the hooves of any potential stray. Jere had told me that cattle were spooked by loud noises or shouting. So there I was, getting mud splattered on my pristine whites, waving a long branch in each hand, whispering to the cattle as they went by me, "Go ahead, you big bastards, keep moving, keep moving," until they were all in the corral.

One experience dichotomized for me a basic difference in eastern and western sensibility. More specifically, urban compared to rural. After breakfast, I was in the front yard and saw Jere's horses going down the driveway, heading toward the main road. I rushed inside, yelling, "The horses are out! The horses are out!" Jere's nose was buried in the *Wall Street Journal* and he was having a cup of coffee and a cigarette, his morning ritual. He paid me no attention. So I ran back outside and chased the horses down the road. All I managed to do was drive them to the fence of the neighboring ranch. Frustrated and feeling totally inadequate, I looked back to see Jere calmly getting into his pickup. He drove over to where his horses were nuzzling the neighbor's horses across the fence, and without getting out of his truck, quietly herded them back home. He locked them into one of the pastures, then ambled back inside the house to continue perusing how his stocks were doing and finish his coffee and cigarette.

It was foreign to my upbringing as well as my nature to accomplish any task by taking things so in stride. But some of Jere's way of being came to rub off on me.

Whenever we pleased, we'd take off for a week or two, driving around the West. Jere had a camper body for his pickup that provided somewhat cramped but cozy lodging. Early on, though, I realized that Jere, having bought our groceries, expected me to cook all our meals in that camper. I didn't mind doing some cooking, but there was a limit. Finally, one day I set him straight. "Jere, enough is enough. I will no longer be a captive cook in a camper kitchen." From then on, it was breakfasts and snacks by my hand, with dinners out.

One evening, Jere and I pulled into a campground and he picked a likely spot. Soon there was a knock at the door. "Who's there?" It was the local sheriff, wanting to know if we had our own toilet. "Are you self-contained?" he asked. I whispered to Jere, "Tell him yes. We hardly ever argue." To which he responded, "You're such a wise ass."

Another time, Jere decided that in the camper we'd follow the 49er Gold Rush mountain road way up to Hangdog Junction, almost to the Nevada border. It turned out there was nothing left of the place but a broken down shack and an old dog. We didn't see its owner. Perhaps the poor dog didn't have one. Coming back down the mountain, Jere seemed to be driving a bit too fast. He assured me, though, he just wanted to get back before dark, and I shouldn't worry. When we got to level ground, he pulled over, his hands shaking, and said, "I need a drink—bad. We've been going down this mountain with no brakes at all!" He'd been swerving from side to side just to keep the camper

83

from turning over. We were lucky that we weren't killed.

On our way to the Grand Canyon, Jere turned to me and asked if I'd like to see Canyon de Chelly, where the Navajos eventually settled. Thinking it would be a slight diversion, I said sure. He turned at the next intersection and we drove 400 miles to that "little side trip." Being a westerner, Jere was used to driving through the wide open spaces without a second thought.

But wanderlust had infected us to the extent that we couldn't be contented, even by the magnificent West. We both wanted to do some serious travelling out of the country. As an easterner, all I knew was to head for Europe; but Jere had other ideas. We were soon off into the world at large like a couple of old teenagers, aged sixty-two and sixty-eight. By the time we were through nearly a decade had passed.

Mexico and Central America

Our first trip was from San Francisco to the Panama Canal by native bus and sometimes passenger trains. We were close to the people and the poverty of Central America. Mexico to Guatemala to Honduras to El Salvador to Costa Rica to Panama. We had no reservations anyplace; we were travelers, not tourists. Where we'd lay our heads each night was a daily adventure. We didn't eat in hotel restaurants, instead following the crowds on the streets to where the locals dined. Sometimes we bought food from street braziers. We trusted the food of the locals as long as it was well cooked. We commonly ate soups because they'd been boiled. Jere drank a lot of beer, while I tended toward coffee.

One day, we walked into a small family-owned restaurant in Antigua, Guatemala for a snack. We only ordered soup, but when the food arrived we discovered that the woman had cooked us an entire meal. Jere, who was fluent in Spanish, told her we really only wanted some soup, but she urged us to eat this feast she'd prepared. She then charged us the exorbitant amount of five dollars American. In broken Spanish, I told her that nowhere else in the world would we be charged so much for a meal that we didn't even order. I was the object of her volley of indignant, rapid-fire

85

Spanish, to which I shrugingly responded, *"No com-prende."* She turned to Jere and asked, "How come sometimes she understands and sometimes she does-n't?" I told Jere, "Just pay the bill and let's leave. Don't even look back." For all I know, that woman is yelling still. Years later, when we reviewed our world travels, Jere and I agreed that our favorite country south of the border had been Guatemala, with its (mostly) gentle Mayan people.

Surrounded by mountains, Lake Atitlan in Guatemala is comparable in beauty to Lake Tahoe in California and Nevada, with the additional interest of an exotic culture. Like Tahoe, Atitlan is a teardrop in the eye of God. A glorious place.

There was a town at the lakeside, so popular with American tourists to be called Gringo Tanango, gringo town. It's real name was Panachal. To go down to Lake Atitlan there was breathtaking. We both wanted to see the villages across the lake, but Jere was chatting up a young American woman. I could see he was enamored of her, and I knew we'd miss the ferry. Sure enough, we never made it to the other side of the lake. I just explored Gringo Tanango on my own while Jere was winding down his flirtation.

The highlight of the trip for me was our journey from Escapulas, way up in the corner of Guatemala, to Honduras. We had arrived in Escapulas on Christmas day. We were in time to see pilgrims ceremoniously dressed in flowing robes, carrying staffs, and wearing wide-brimmed hats covered with flowers, fruits, and vegetables, *a la* Carmen Miranda. They were wending their way into the church to make tribute to various saints. The most popular statue was of a black Christ;

there were throngs around it. The white Christ had few supplicants. I've always felt that fervent prayers to Mary would get Jesus to act quickly. Because she was a Jewish mother, she would've nagged Him until He got done whatever she wanted. Jere and I noticed that we were the only ones who turned around and walked out of the church. Everyone else shuffled out respectfully backward, as local tradition dictated.

The next morning, we hopped on a mini-bus. In addition to picking up passengers, the driver was the local postman, and he stopped all along his route to drop off and pick up mail. He nodded his head, agreeably it seemed, when we said we were going to Honduras. We settled back for a relaxing trip, until the driver suddenly stopped, telling us that he had delivered all his mail and wasn't going any farther. He dropped us off in a little, one-street village in the middle of nowhere, still far from the Honduran border.

"Jere, what do we do now?"

" I'm going to get a beer," he replied. Jere drank his beer, then stretched out on the non-sidewalk, using his suitcase as a pillow. "Something will happen," he said, as he closed his eyes for a snooze.

I was left to commiserate with a tiny Mayan woman and her two tiny children, who were also stranded there. "No desayuno," (No breakfast) she said to me, pointing to her children. Since I always carried a little comfort food with me, I was able to at least give her sugared fruit for her kids. When they had finished, I gave her a tissue as well. She said to me in Spanish, "Thank you. You have everything." I thought, *Yes, compared to so many other people, Americans do have everything.* In broken Spanish and impromptu sign language we understood each other quite well. And we had something in common: We all wanted to get over the border into Honduras, she to her home, and us to Copan, the site of Mayan ruins.

Then we saw a minivan coming up the road in the direction we wanted to go. I jumped up and stood squarely in the middle of the road. The driver had the choice of running me over, or stopping.

Later on, I asked him, "Why did you stop?"

"You looked desperate. Besides, I didn't want to get any dents."

As we were boarding the minivan, Jere whispered to me, "Don't say a word." I quickly realized why. The van was full of well-dressed American tourists who most likely had paid plenty for their trip to Guatemala, and who now found themselves sharing their expensive tranportation with a couple of travel bums.

At the Honduran border, we all presented our passports and continued on to the little town of Copan. The fat cat tourists and the two of us rolled up to the same hotel, were assigned rooms in the same drought situation (no water for showers), and ate in the same restaurant. They gave us disdainful glances, but didn't have any more comfort than we did, in spite of their pseudo-superiority. It was we who met with the mayor of the town since Jere was the only one of the whole bunch who spoke Spanish.

The ruins of Copan had been only partially excavated, and I realized that the hillocks in the fields were unearthed middens. My biggest thrill there was signing my name in the museum register just below the signature of the famous Norwegian anthropologist and explorer Thor Heyerdahl. About a quarter century before, he and his crew had braved the broad Pacific in the Kon Tiki, proving that it was possible for South American natives to sail from Chile all the way to Melanesia in a balsa wood raft.

The poverty in Central America was appalling. Costa Rica was the most comfortable for us of all the Central American countries, and in political, economic, and social terms, it was the closest to our own American standard of living of any place we visited on that trip. Honduras and Nicaragua were sorry sights, obviously exploited by morally bankrupt politicians and devastated by earthquakes. In Managua in 1977, only two buildings remained untouched by recent earthquakes. One was the ten-story Bank of America building, and the other was the local police compound. We didn't linger there for long.

In Panama, we had no choice but to register at a commercial hotel instead of a family-run lodging, which we would've preferred. We spent a happy day and a half at the Mira Flora locks of the Panama Canal, sitting way up high and looking down at the ships entering and leaving. It was as if the walls of the locks were moving up and down, but actually the water rose and lowered to meet sea level (what did I know from locks without cream cheese and bagels?) Enormous steamers and freighters would come in, and if another boat, even a small yacht, could still be squeezed into a lock it would be. When the water level reached the commensurate level with the water outside the locks, the vessels sailed through safely. What an intriguing solution for passage across land from the Caribbean to the Pacific.

We rode the rails from west to east and back again

across Panama, parallel to the canal. I bought several molas, which were multi-colored squares of cloth. Panamanian women would cut through layers of different colored cloths to create the traditional designs of the Cuna Indians. Instead of adding bits and patches of cloth, the designs were made by cutting layers away. Then these cuts were carefully hand-hemmed. The women used the molas for blouses and skirts.

Yucatan was the last stop of our two-month trip. We flew into the city of Merida in Mexico, near the Mayan ruins of Chichenitza. I started to climb the steep steps inside one of the pyramids, but the ceilings were so low and the steps so short that I backed out before I got very far in out of claustrophobia. Choc Mal, the Mayan god, was depicted with his body facing forward and his head backward, for some reason we never learned. Jere and I saw earnest archeologists sweating away in the heat as they carefully whisked away dust from the bases of pedestals and columns that had supported structures long gone. While other eager auslanders were busily climbing ruins all around us, Jere and I were prudent in the hot weather and lazy enough to sit quietly in the shade.

In Merida, we rode bumpy trolley cars without springs in the seats. I couldn't help but contrast this with my memories of taking the trolley from Belle Harbor to high school in Far Rockaway. Quite a difference for this New York girl. The bone-crunching discomfort of the ride in Merida, though, was offset by the wonderfully exotic sights out the window.

Having spread our wings for the first time together outside our own country, we happily flew KLM from Merida to Mexico City, then back to San

Francisco. Sixty days down by native bus, six hours back by air. I'd sent sixty postcards, one a day, to Christine, and had in my luggage a bag full of little dolls representing the costumes of each country Jere and I had visited.

South America

Our next trip took us just a bit farther, to South America. Avianca Airlines deposited us in Bogota, Columbia, and our well laid plans hit a snag right off the bat. As soon as I saw our luggage I knew something was amiss.

"Don't touch that suitcase!" I said to Jere. "I can tell it's been tampered with. We'll only open it in the presence of the airport manager."

Sure enough, it had been burgled. Several items of clothing were missing, along with my binoculars. I happened to mention to the airport manager that we were going to visit Senor Gomez in Popayan, when suddenly everyone around us jumped to attention. I didn't realize until a couple of weeks later that Senor Gomez was one of the most powerful businessmen in Columbia. (Gomez is not his real name—frankly, I don't remember his real name!)

My son Bill had known Senor Gomez's son in the Bay Area. Bill had written ahead on our behalf, and Senor Gomez had extended an invitation to Jere and me to visit his finca (ranch) as well as his home in Popayan.

The airport manager asked me to estimate the value of what had been stolen so that Avianca could reimburse us, which the company did. I wrestled with my conscience, but for the inconvenience to us and lax security on the part of the airline, I asked for three times what the binoculars were worth. But they would've given ten times that amount once they knew that we had a connection with Senor Gomez. It was certainly nice to have money in pocket that we hadn't expected.

I was impressed with the magnificent architecture of the high-rises in the center of Bogota; more beautiful, I thought, than what one sees in New York City. In visiting the museum in Bogota, I discovered that Columbians have a deep sense of design, aesthetics, and fine art. One imaginative expression of social conditions that we saw was a construction four or five feet high, entirely of worn-out shoes: a pyramid of the hardship of common folk.

In the eateries and on the streets, I noticed that the men all wore trousers that were so tight no pickpocket could insert even a single finger into the pockets to steal anything. Jere and I found it amusing to watch variations of this silent defense against thievery as we sat at breakfast sipping *tinto*, demitase cups of dark Columbian coffee.

Morning after morning from our hotel window, we saw two little donkeys plodding unescorted down the street, wending their way through heavy traffic and crossing a thoroughfare as wide as Broadway, with no one guiding them. I still wonder about those seemingly self-directed donkeys. Were they wandering aimlessly, or were they perhaps transporting cocaine from hither to yon? I'll never know.

Jere and I did a lot of bus travel around Bogota. One day, as we were about to board a bus, we found ourselves surrounded by a group of women and children. Gentlemanly as always, Jere let them get on ahead of him. Some got on ahead, and some pushed him onto the bus from behind, effectively separating the two of us. By the time we got off the bus, the women and children had all disappeared—and Jere discovered that his wallet had also disappeared. I suggested that we buy him some of those defensively tight pants worn by the locals, but he preferred to just be more mindful while staying with the wardrobe he'd brought.

We went to an exhibition of folk art that included exquisite textiles, ceramics, paintings, and macrame. We were about to leave when the woman in charge yelled, "Don't go out! There's a pickpocket outside waiting for you."

"Sure you don't want to reconsider those tight pants?" I asked Jere.

"No way."

"I think you'd look kinda sexy in 'em."

"Old dog, new tricks. Forget about it."

"At least consider using that zippered pouch I bought for you in Guadalajara."

"Not my style, Frances."

We looked outside and saw nobody at all. But the store proprietress insisted that we remain inside until she called the police.

A policeman arrived promptly and escorted us out and across the park. Jere asked him, "Where's the pickpocket?"

"Over there," said the policeman, pointing to a woman in sneakers, who looked to be in her late seventies, sitting under a tree.

"But that's just a harmless old woman!" I exclaimed.

"Harmless as a scorpion," the policeman said. "She's made herself rich from unsuspecting tourists."

Ours not to reason why. Ours but to do or die... or be complete suckers. We came to find out that the only time we were safe from thievery in Columbia was when Carnival was going on in Brazil. Every pick-pocket worth his or her salt would be down there working overtime.

From Bogota, we took a dust bowl relic of a bus southeast to the city of Popayan, stopping at Tierra Dente to visit archeological sites; strange little stone houses thousands of years old with concave roofs still intact. After two dusty days, we arrived at Popayan, got a room in a pension, and called Senora Gomez. It was a difficult conversation as I spoke little Spanish and she spoke even less English. Somehow, though, I under-stood that we were invited to lunch at their home.

The meal was bland, rice, vegetables, and chicken. Jere, speaking fluent Spanish, got along fine. But for me it was an awkward lunch of smiles and meaning-less pleasant nods. The Gomez house was large, con-servatively furnished, much like an American middle-class home. We were impressed that the property was surrounded by an eight-foot-high wrought-iron fence and closely watched over by armed guards. The more someone has, the more has to be protected—reason to avoid becoming wealthy, ha-ha. In the courtyard were parked several large trucks and farm equipment: reapers and harvesters. Why here rather than out at the Gomez's ranch? Simple: It was too hard to provide security out in the open finca.

The next day, we traveled with Senora Gomez and her friend to their finca, about fifteen miles outside of Popayan. It was a hundred acres or so, with four houses, and sheep pastures. Senor Gomez, who spoke fairly fluent English, took Jere and me to see the pasture that was a particular source of our host's pleasure and pride. Growing amid the tall sugarcane were tiny, foothigh redwood trees that Senor Gomez had brought back from Northern California. The most enjoyment we had during the day and a half we spent on the finca was our midday siesta; otherwise, it was the unrelieved boredom of witnessing the complacency of the idle rich.

We returned with Senora Gomez and her friend to Popayan in a cloudburst, with Senora Gomez constantly singing to "El Senor." It took me awhile to figure out that she was praying to Jesus to get us back safely. Jere and I were glad to get back to our pension, free from the constraint of obligatory sociability.

The next time Jere was pickpocketed in Columbia was in the city of Pasto, near the Equadorian border. As we approached the bus after our lunch stop, it was obvious that Jere had been stung. His shirt was unbuttoned and wide open. He thought he'd outfoxed all pickpockets by keeping his wallet out of his pockets and under his belt. Wrong. Jere finally admitted that he must be a walking target, and agreed to use that zippered pouch I'd given him.

Plunk in the middle of the Andes, about fifty miles south of the Columbia-Equador border is the lovely little town of Otavalo, where we settled into a wonderful place to stay. We lounged in the hotel coffee shop and watched the passing scene on the street, pedestrians, and burros pulling carts. The people stared back at us in mutual curiosity. We must've looked strange in our American-style clothes, and they were exotic to us in their ponchos and rebozos. We were all just folks taking in each other's cultures.

At the open-air market, Jere counted twenty-eight varieties of potatoes, a product, he informed me, that was of New World origin. Ironic, it seemed to us, how the Irish came to America in such droves due to their potato famine, for lack of a food that had originated in the New World.

I loved the wall hangings made of alpaca fur, with designs of llamas and dancing figures stitched in heavy thread. Once, we saw a woman leading her husband down the street to the market. He was so laden down with straw baskets that he couldn't see his way. All we could see of him were his legs moving ahead under the humongous load of baskets.

My life turned around one night at dinnertime when, for the first time, I heard the haunting tones of Andean music played on pipes, charangos, and drums. Those intriguing tones have become the fiber of my musical being. To me, they are the most yearning, beautiful sounds in the world, the essence of nature. The strains were more captivating even than my beloved Brahms, Bach, Beethoven, or the Americana compositions of Aaron Copeland. This indigenous music is to me the sounds of unspoken, unuttered humanity trying to draw into our bodies the secrets of earth and sky.

We traveled south from Otavalo to the city of Quito. All my life I'd looked forward to being in Quito, but once there I hated it because it was so crowded.

Jere liked the teeming masses since he had lived almost his whole life on a ranch. But for me, having grown up in and around New York City, crowds were all too familiar and unwelcome. I was disillusioned to find the streets so mobbed. And it frightened me to see gun-toting militia on the streets, challenging striking, shouting students. Jere and I were amused when we walked into a section of the city where on one street each house had its own ersatz Spanish, French, or Renaissance Italian design. It was a crazy, tasteless display of wealth and architectural incongruities.

We took a bus up to a midpoint in the city that was right on the equator. You could stand with one foot in the northern hemisphere and the other in the southern. Blowing in the wind up there was the unmistakable smell of marijuana.

From Quito, we continued on to the seaport of Guayaquil and caught a ferry out to the Galapagos Islands, home of masses of huge tortoises and blue-gray sea iguanas. And I thought Quito was congested! Compared to these creatures packed together on the beaches, a Brooklyn tenement would seem sparsely populated. Iguanas, mild-mannered monsters, so deceptively dangerous looking, would come out of the water to nibble the crumbs from under our breakfast and dinner tables. They paddled in the waves and allowed us to swim along with them. As their smooth scaly forms would rub against my skin I couldn't help but think what a contrast this was from swimming in the surf in Rockaway. In a lot of ways, I was getting more daring in my later years.

Sometimes the larger iguanas would come up on the sand, stretch their forelegs into the cactus clusters, and pull off the spiny leaves to eat. Jere and I explored around the island, observing the giant tortoises. We took note of the distinctive patterns on their shells, specific, we were told, to the island where each tortoise had originated. The tortoises were big, and lumbered along at no miles per hour, so it was easy to approach them and identify these designs.

While visiting the Galapagos, I was offered a job teaching English, but I declined. As enchanting as it was, I couldn't quite imagine calling this place home for much more than the week we spent there. But it was a good week among the native Equadorians who, like us, were there on vacation, and we had lots of fun ferrying between the islands. Being seasoned travelers, Jere and I stuck to eating fish, freshly caught, with potatoes, and popcorn, staples of the Equadorian diet. We avoided imported meats and vegetables. When sailing between islands, we chose boats with younger passengers, merrily disco-dancing the evenings away. Middle aged, conservative older folks on the other boats watched with maybe a bit of envy as this aging East Coast teacher and her rancher beau kicked up our heels. They nicknamed Jere, "the cowboy, Juan Juain."

Two young women boat passengers invited us to their home city of Cuenca. We dined with them one evening at a restaurant. I was expecting the normal eatery hubbub, but when we arrived we were ushered into a private room. It was supposed to feel invitingly exclusive, but I found it disappointing. We were served a local delicacy, guinea pig, which tasted sweet and good, but I felt sorry crunching down on their delicate little bones. It was even sadder for me than when I had eaten rabbit. Poor defenseless creatures.

I had lent one of our young friends my polyester sweater, and she hadn't yet returned it, so I bought an Equadorian shawl, a striking handwoven garment that I still wear. But, by the time Jere and I arrived in Cuenca, I had been going native for so long that I'd begun to want something American to remind me of home. One day, near the end of our stay in this town, I spotted an ice cream store with multi-colored plastic tables and chairs. I immediately satisfied the familiarity I'd been craving. You never know what will offset a little homesickness.

From Cuenca, we flew to Lima, Peru. Here we noticed that Jere was frequently being asked for the time. Eventually, we figured out that there was little concern for punctuality, rather thieves just wanted to ascertain if his watch was worth stealing. Poor Jere, he was coming to believe that he might as well have worn a sandwich board with "victim" posted on both sides.

We went to see Pizarro's skeleton in the national museum. The catacombs under the museum contained room after room of bones: a room full of hip bones, one filled with arm bones, another of skulls, all separated with orthopedic exactitude. The bones were so old and brown they weren't even gruesome seeming, just historical.

There is a big deal made in Lima over the changing of the guard at the royal palace each day at noon. I was anxious to see this spectacle as one of the highlights of our visit. The marching band played with great fanfare, but the guards were all out of step. Just goes to show, practice doesn't necessarily make perfect.

The next day, we went to the tourist bureau and thereupon found our way over the Andes by plane to the city of Arequipa. Here we indulged ourselves by taking rooms in a commercial hotel instead of a pension or other more humble lodgings. We thought we were due for the comfort of a shower, clean sheets, and a certain amount of privacy. We visited an ancient Catholic convent with its own swimming pool, in which long ago nuns bathed fully clothed. They must've felt that cleanliness was not quite as close to godliness as modesty. We discovered a wonderful local drink, pisco sours, which we imbibed morning, noon, and night. We were high and happy, spending our time comparing adventures with fellow travelers.

During our second night in Arequipa, tranquility was shattered by an earthquake that cut off the electricity and hot water in our hotel. So much for our well-deserved luxuries. What a hub-bub in the central bus station the next day! It seemed like the whole city was talking about the unsettling experience of the night before. In the hustle-bustle of getting off a telegram to Bill in San Francisco to let him know that we were safe, I found that my handbag had been neatly sliced and my change purse slipped out with the delicacy of a skilled surgeon. Jere finally had victim company. I lost twenty dollars and an identification card, but I always kept important papers on me, so nothing of great value was gone. I ended up phoning instead of sending a wire, because there was such a mob scene at the telegraph office. When I finally got Bill on the line, his response was, "What earthquake?" What was big news in Peru wasn't even known about in the States.

We traveled to the ancient town of Cuzco, way up in the Andes by publico, a sort of outsized taxi cab

101

holding six or eight passengers. When we checked into our lodgings, we ordered a cup of tea. Floating in the tea when it arrived was a coca leaf, the purpose of which was to help us adjust to the high altitude, about 14,000 feet. Cuzco was a small enough place to be convenient for walking around. It was quite old, founded thousands of years before by the Incas, inhabited now mostly by their descendents. We saw so many whitewashed stucco houses, with blue doorways and window frames and red tile roofs that we almost were inclined to salute. Women wore colorful serapes and the men draped themselves with ponchos, the height of Peruvian style.

I've never been much for souvenirs, but I bought a wall hanging of Inca musicians. I also purchased a watercolor by a local artist of a street scene in Cuzco, of women running uphill, weaving as they ran, that hangs on the wall of my bedroom to this day. In and around the city we saw women hurrying up and down the hills, all the while spinning and winding yarn on spindles. They ran up those hills as if climbing them was no effort at all.

We took a train to its last stop, then went by rickety bus even higher into the mountains to get to Macchu Picchu. The grade was so steep that the road was in switchbacks, zigging and zagging all the way to the site. The stone walls outlined houses and rooms within houses, their roofs long gone. No one has ever solved the mystery of the purpose of these structures, or of the remarkable masonry techniques that made stone fit to stone tightly, without the slightest gaps. The atmosphere of this mysterious place lent itself to silence; even having a meal in the restaurant took on an eerie quality. Jere and I regretted that we hadn't arranged to stay there overnight because we found the ambiance so mysterious and magical. The location of Macchu Picchu is high above the tree line, and there's no other human settlement even remotely nearby. It was set in a stunningly desolate landscape.

Our next destination was La Paz, in neighboring Bolivia. Jere asked me, "Why do you want to go there?"

"What did Hillary say about climbing Everest?" I answered Socratically. Sir Edmund Hillary was drawn to Mount Everest and I was drawn to La Paz. I told Jere that since we were in the neighborhood, I just wanted to see Bolivia, home of tin, as had been drummed into me in school. The take-off point over Lake Titicaca—highest navigable body of water in the world—was the little town of Puno, on the Peruvian side of the lake. I vividly remember the candelaria, a celebration of dancing, singing, and brass bands playing. True to the Peruvian way, the bands played out of tune, but with much gusto.

Just offshore from Puno were floating reed islands where fishermen lived. Their single-sailed boats were constructed of the same reeds that made up the islands themselves. We bought tickets for the overnight trip across the lake to La Paz. Naïve as we were, we assumed that with these first-class tickets we'd have first-class accomodations. Nothing doing. The steward showed us to a four-bunk room that we were expected to share with two young men. "Oh, no," I said. "We're not sharing a room with those men." With a grand flourish, the indignant steward took out his key, locked the room, and dramatically announced that if we wouldn't share a room we'd have nowhere to sleep for the night.

In the ship's dining room that evening, we met another couple, Bob and Carol from Wisconsin. They were in the same sleeping quarter predicament, so we swapped roommates and bunked together. None of us undressed that night. The four of us each tossed and turned in our uncomfortable bunks. All night long, I heard the clink of coins falling out of Jere's pockets onto the floor. We all wondered how much worse second-class could've been.

On the Bolivian side of the lake, the train was crammed with travelers. Rising high above us was flat-topped Sugarloaf Mountain, and way up on the summit was La Paz. Bob and Carol went off to a standard American hotel full of fellow countrymen. But we'd had our luxury fix in Arequipa, so we settled into a small hotel that catered mostly to locals. As far as we were concerned, when in Rome...

We stayed on Manco Capek Street, one side with commercial buildings, the other side dominated by a stone wall that looked and smelled like it had been peed on from time immemorial. One outstanding memory I have of La Paz is of the well-dressed Cechua women on a holiday outing, wearing their bowler hats (derbies) and flowing, brown velvet dresses and jackets. We didn't do much walking around the city because the streets were much too steep and the air too thin. I dearly wanted to see the streets where all the herbs were sold, although I just didn't think I had the breath for it and neither did Jere.

One day, Jere said that he wanted to walk farther down the street to get cigarettes. I said that I'd wait for him, but it took him so long that I was reminded of a scene in a play in which a character was described as having gone down to get a pack of cigarettes and his family didn't see him again for a couple of years. I had no such concerns with Jere, but growing tired of waiting, I walked back to our hotel. On the way, I was fantasizing how wonderful it would be to bite into a big juicy hamburger. A relapse of homesickness.

Returning to Peru after a stay in La Paz of a few days, we took the railroad, skirting Lake Titicaca. In Puno, we caught a publico with four other passengers and it took us all the way across the country. It was a pretty straight run because the driver had no choice but to keep his car in the ruts of the dirt road. They guided that publico as surely as tracks keep a train on course. Vegetation was sparse and scrubby. The countryside looked like a moonscape, except for the young boys on bicycles herding their llamas.

After about three hours, we stopped for lunch at a restaurant in a stone hut. As we stepped over the threshold I realized that I was in a setting that would've looked familiar to Fred and Wilma Flintstone. Jere and I ordered a delicious vegetable soup, but one of the young women we were traveling with ordered meat, which made her sick for the rest of the hours-long ride to Lima. After the meal, I asked the proprietor where the bathroom was. He led me outdoors and gestured widely to a long, ancient stone wall as if to say, "Wherever you like."

We stayed in Lima just long enough to find out that there were landslides occurring all over the area. We took that as a sign that it was time to return home. Discretion being the better part of valor and, especially

105

after the earthquake in Arequipa, I didn't want to risk further travel in South America. But, looking back, I only wish we could've gone south along the coast to see the timeless and mysterious Nazco Lines, paths of patterned markings extending for miles along the coastal plain. They reveal themselves most clearly from the air, leading to speculation that extra terrestrials had made the lines on a visit long, long ago. Who knows?

The trip had been two months of unique adventure and yielded many subsequent years of interesting, warm memories. When you're on a traveler's trek you run into many discomforts. Once back home, though, the negatives tend to fade in time, while the memories grow even fonder.

I wolfed down my longed-for hamburger on the first day I was back. But soon I was in for a gastronomical treat beyond compare.

Photos

Frances and Joe, age 38.
Playland, Rockaway Beach.

Frances, age 14, alone in the crowd.
(Top center, cast in shadow.)

High school days, Woodcraft League of America.
Picnicking in Van Cortland Park, NY.
Frances in bottom right corner.

Age 12. Me and my mom.

Billy (6), Amy (1), and me (30) with my hair drawn back
in the unfashionable "Grant Wood" mode.

Ana Lief (my mother). Always popular with her nieces and nephews for her goodies and wisecracks.

A day at the beach. What could be sweeter? Frances (26), Joe (26), and little Billy (3). I'm chewing on sea grass.

Frances (20's) on the porch.

Summer vacation, Mt. Tremper, New York, 1945.
Frances (30), Joe (30), Amy (1), Billy (5).

Ana Lief (82) blessing the Sabbath candles, 1952.
Billy took this photograph.

Amy (7) wishing she was somewhere else than the Bronx Zoo.

Amy (4) and Bill (9).

My niece Faith, Bill, Frances and Jere
at the Alta Mia Restauant in Sausalito, CA (1978).

Frances and Joe (1970) at the sea shore, Atlantic Beach, Long Island.

Joe Thompson, Nina Farnia, Michael Feinstein,
and me at a Hallinan Fundraiser.

Frances (85) in a naughty mode listening to David's
"sweet nothings." San Francisco, CA.

Frances and David Steinberg (1998).

Jere's 70th Birthday

Back at the ranch, we settled down for the time being. No trips planned for the immediate future. I looked at Jere one night and said, "Your seventieth birthday is coming up."

"Don't rub it in."

"We should have a party. You're only seventy once."

"Hmmm. Been awhile since I've had a... major barbecue."

And that it was.

A month before the event, Jere and his daughter Inez sent out about 200 invitations to their rancher neighbors. I invited my family and friends from San Francisco. It was to be a curious and interesting cultural mix.

What I'd had in mind to serve were bowls of spaghetti, as I would've done back on Dashby Court. But we were far west of there—Jere's idea was better. He decided to have two lambs butchered, dressed out, and baked in the earth the old-fashioned way. My job was to prepare the dressing, which I researched as thoroughly as if I were going to do a dissertation on the subject. After all, I was kind of an interloper in this California ranch crowd and I didn't want to screw up. My culinary responsibility, though, turned out to be pleasantly simple. One lamb was filled with apples that had been rolled in cinnamon. The other lamb was stuffed with rice. Jere and I ate different preparations of rice for a month until our palates passed favorable judgment on a savory sweet flavor of allspice, salt, mushrooms, and onions.

Jere and a few of his neighbors dug a couple of three-foot-deep pits in the yard with backhoes. The pits were stacked, first with paper and kindling, then split fruitwood logs. "A rule of the axe" is to figure on wood enough to have a stack three times the volume of the pit. Once the fire was going, logs were added until there was a bed of red hot coals a couple of feet or so in depth. This took about six hours. The coals were raked level. Then, gravel was shoveled over them, just enough so that the glow of the coals showed through. The lambs were wrapped in old bedsheets and lowered into the pit with heavy wire, which had handles at the ends for easy extraction when cooking was done. Corrugated tin sheets were placed on top of the pit, and a mound of dirt shoveled over that. The mound was watered down by a garden hose to seal the "oven." Steam leaks popping through would be quickly covered with more dirt. What amazed me about the process was that there was no apparent oxygen to keep the coals burning. But nature and time testing has its way, so in about another eight hours, if memory serves, the lambs were cooked to perfection.

In addition to the lambs, we had a whole pig grilled slowly on a rotisserie. The meat was richly flavorful, the "crackling" skin thick and moist.

We had at least twenty tables set out in the pasture. The event was partially pot luck and our guests served themselves, not only these succulent barbecued meats, but vegetables, salsas, bread, muffins, salads, and fruit pies. Wine and beer flowed freely. Inez had ordered a huge birthday flat cake. There were far less than seventy candles, though. Being a smoker of long standing, it's doubtful that Jere could have worked up the breath to blow out that many.

Symbolic of the diversity of our guests, an impression that stays with me is that the country folk all drove up in shiny, brand-new cars, while those I knew from San Francisco arrived in older, beat-up models. This could be an exaggeration of memory. But everyone, no matter how little they might've had in common, all seemed to blend amazingly well. The party was the thing, and this odd convergence of people were dedicated to just having fun. There were Portuguese, Spanish, Irish, and Oklahomans represented. But I was probably the only easterner there, a stranger in a strange land. All in all, it seemed to be a grand day.

Most important, I knew that Jere was having the time of his life. He was proud to show my stained glass, and invited several party guests to come into my workshop to see my latest projects in progress.

At one point, I was asked where the bathroom was. I thought it easier to just lead the way than to give directions. After I did, it was said, with a slight degree of irritation, that there was a more direct route. I acknowledged that this was probably true. What I didn't say was that my eyesight had become so poor that by now I only was only able to find my way anywhere with the aid of familiar landmarks.

So much wonderful had happened with me since I'd met Jere. My life had become an adventure of new kinds of people and exotic places. I found it ironic that as my sight was fading, my vision was growing brighter.

Across the Pacific and Down Under

It wasn't long before Jere and I got wanderlust again. This time we decided to head farther west, till it became east—the South Pacific.

I managed to wheedle discount tickets from Continental Airlines by saying that we were "two old folks who were living in 'Last Gasp Gulch.'" As a "Christmas present," according to the seller, we got two roundtrip tickets from San Francisco to Sydney, Australia, including several stopovers along the way, good for two months. Jere and I could hardly pack our bags fast enough.

Our first stop was Hawaii. When we got off the plane in Honolulu, we stepped into a perfumed atmosphere. Wherever the plumerias and gardenias grew, there was a fragrance in the air as alluring as softly strumming ukuleles. We found our way through the city, up to Diamond Head, and all around the island of Oahu for only fifty cents in bus fare, no tourists us— travelers all the time. At the stunning aquarium we viewed countless breeds of tiny, brightly colored fish. Being the avid amateur zoologist that he was, Jere felt at a loss that he couldn't identify many of these pied-patterned, tropical specimens.

A few hours at the Brigham Young University Museum in Honolulu introduced us to the multi-cultures of Polynesia. The highlight of our week was circumnavigating Oahu on native bus. We got off the bus for a quick lunch, and watched gigantic, powerful waves roll in and out. These waves challenge the best of the world's longboard surfers. Some waves must have been twenty feet high. They sure put to shame the piddly ones of Rockaway.

From Hawaii, we flew to American Samoa and checked into the only hotel on the island. It was probably as mildewed and sorry looking as it had been when Somerset Maugham wrote of it in his 1921 short story "Rain," about wanton Sadie Thompson and the righteous man of the cloth who destroyed himself in his obsession with her.

American Samoa is a small island with outsized busses with outsized seats to accommodate the outsized girth of Samoans. We found an inordinate number of people lounging in the streets. The oppressive heat most likely contributed to the general indolence of the community. People at the hotel explained that American Samoa had a weak economy, bolstered by U.S. welfare. My impression was that this money was easily come by, and all anyone had to do was as little as convenient and merely wait for the monthly dole to arrive.

We were urged by the hotel staff to get out of American Samoa, as the real beauty of the islands was in neighboring Western Samoa. We took their advice, and a tiny plane landed Jere and me practically on the grounds of Aggie Gray's International Hotel. Besides rooms at the hotel, there were guest bungalows on the property. It was a restful place to laze the days away, exchanging travel tips and enjoying the best of hospitality.

We took a taxi around the island. Our driver took us to hidden waterfalls and little dwellings tucked safe and dry in hillsides beneath the falls. Western Samoans are a cordial and proud people. They live in an independent nation with a healthy economy, beholden to no other country. Western Samoa is a self-contained island, a place of peace and cultural harmony. No auslander can own land there. Visitors are welcome, but this island country is first and foremost for its citizens, so different from American Samoa.

It was a shock coming to "civilization" on the island of Fiji. It was also an independent country, formerly a British colony, but one that had been spoiled by greed. As when arriving in any new country, we stopped into the airport tourist bureau to find a place to stay, exchange currency, and find out the price of cab fare to our lodging destination. The young cab driver we got took us to our hotel and demanded a fare twice as high as the estimate given at the tourist bureau. We handed him what we understood to be the going rate.

"That's not right," he objected in a surly tone.

"That's what we were told it would be. And its all the money we have" Jere replied.

"If you don't have money, don't come to Fiji."

Hospitality reigned supreme.

The beaches in Fiji, however, have lovely clean sand, and the waters are warm. Our hotel was suitable in all respects but one: The dining room was infested with fleas, so we ate in town. Jere found some welcoming locals at a restaurant who invited him to join them in a drink of kava, a native brew of greeting and acceptance. I wasn't included in the ceremony, since as a woman I was apparently a second class citizen.

Sexism also reigned supreme—not unlike here.

Nandi, the capital of Fiji, was a small town full of entrepreneurs and small businesses. The romance connoted by the name Fiji, in my opinion, exaggerates the island's allures. It was so hot that I had to buy a lightweight dress, made for me on the spot in about a half an hour at a yard goods store. I chose a typical indigenous pattern, and I still have that dress. When I wear it these days, people often remark on the uniqueness of the design, a black and white geometric pattern.

I wanted to rinse out a few undergarments, but discovered that we had no clothesline on which to dry them. A resourceful chambermaid solved the problem by ripping up one of our sheets, braiding the lengths of cloth, and stringing the makeshift rope outside our window. That clothesline traveled with us all over the Pacific. Mostly we used it for its original intention, but we once used it to tie up Jere's suitcase that had a broken lock, and another time the cloth rope secured our luggage to a pushcart. It remained a much appreciated souvenir of ingenuity. I've wondered if that chambermaid learned sheet braiding in a prison escape.

Leaving Fiji, we flew to Aukland, New Zealand. Landing at the airport, we hoped we would be able to distinguish Jere's cousins, whom he had never met. They made it easy for us, ready with a sign boldly labeled "Jere." He and his female cousin looked like two peas out of the same pod, both blond Scandinavians.

Our adventure with Jere's cousin Nancy and her husband Ted started with a few days spent at their home. They lived in the main house with their youngest child. There were three other houses on the property, each occupied by one or more of their other kids (Since Jere also had four houses on his ranch, I speculated that this could be a Swedish thing). There were Nan's children, Ted's children, and the youngest child, whom they'd had together. A rule of the family was that when guests came to stay, the youngest would give up his room and move in with one of his siblings. Jere and I were quartered in a room with a *mal de mer* inducing waterbed and walls covered with young adult-themed posters of outrageously costumed rock stars.

Jere, his cousins, and I took off on a five-day trip around New Zealand's North Island, the smaller of the country's two main islands. The most remarkable thing I remember about the North Island were the kauri trees, as big around and tall as California redwoods and even more ancient. Walking amid the kauri trees brought a peaceful, almost spiritual feeling.

We rode the ferry on the Bay of Islands as it delivered mail. It would come fairly close to shore and a deckhand would extend a long rod to which was attached a basket for delivering or picking up mail. It was a trick for the people of the island to catch hold of the rod. They called it the flying fox.

Many of the Maoris, who are the natives of New Zealand, live in a territory called Rotorua. It's the home of thermal geysers, steaming lakes of bubbling mud, and sulfur hot springs, many of which have been diverted into manmade pools. Jere and I rented a private sulfur hot tub. We couldn't stay in it for more than a few minutes because the water was so hot and penetrating. We emerged spent from the heat, but feeling squeaky clean.

132

Song and dance shows recounting the history of their Polynesian origins were staged by the Maoris for tourists. Although we didn't understand the Maoris' language, we could comprehend the drama of their body language (as long as I was up close enough to see), which told of the winds and the weather and their travel across the South Pacific to New Zealand. Earlier, in Aukland, we had seen a display demonstrating the seaworthiness of the large Maori canoes, which held up to seventy-some people. It was the Maoris who first settled the South Island.

New Zealand's South Island struck us as quite different from the more developed North Island. For the most part, it was more entrepreneurial with cities and many shops. There were neat, well-ordered guest cottages, where it was the responsibility of every guest to clean up and prepare the cottage for the next occupant. The accent of the South Islanders is incomprehensible. In traveling around, we needed to pay strict attention to where we were because, although they were in some form of English, seemingly an offshoot of cockney, we could hardly understand spoken directions. In one railroad station, we observed two conductors who looked like Tweedle-Dee and Tweedle-Dum. In calling out train arrivals and destinations, their heavy-starched dialects out-Britished the British.

The Canterbury Plains, about midway down the South Island, led to a coastline cut with deep fjords. We took a boat across one of them, and it rained so hard that in minutes we were drenched. We were surrounded by water around us, above us, and below us. When we docked, the captain let on that we had been in a dangerous situation that caused him more than a little

133

concern. But innocent as we were of local weather haz-
ards, we'd thoroughly enjoyed our soaking, as we
watched water thundering down the fjord into the bay.

Jere always took great pains to schedule our trips
for times when the local climates would be favorable.
But during the season we visited New Zealand he'd
miscalculated a bit. It was so unbelievably wet. During
our three-week stay on the South Island, it rained vir-
tually every day. I used layers of clothing until there
was nothing left in my suitcase to wear. Later, in
describing our time there, I said that it had rained
twenty-two days out of our twenty-one day stay.

The most uncomfortable part of our trip to New
Zealand was having to endure a group of Australians
on a bus tour who had gotten it into their heads that
they hated Americans. In all our nine years of traveling
together, I was only twice aware of blatant discrimina-
tion against us. One time was crossing from Costa Rica
into Panama, being brushed aside in the ladies room
by a couple of black tourists who determined that I
was white trash. The second time was with those
Aussies on that bus. What saved my dignity was
understanding the dynamics of the situation, so that I
wasn't sad or hurt or even angry. I simply needed to be
patient and remind myself, "this, too, shall pass."

The Christchurch Museum, largely devoted to the
history of Antarctic exploration, held the secrets,
adventures, hardships, fears, and equipment—sleds,
parkas, dog harnesses, etc.—of Richard Byrd's expedi-
tion to the South Pole. I walked around that museum
holding my breath with excitement. If not for a terrible
airplane accident over Antarctica a few months before
we arrived in New Zealand, Jere and I would surely

have opted for a flight over the South Pole. Instead, we compromised with a plane ride over Mt. Cook, New Zealand's highest peak. We landed way up on the mountain and stepped out onto virgin snow; quite a contrast to the warm weather a few thousand feet below.

On the whole, we found New Zealand to be a country of shopkeepers and farmers who are fiercely proud of their fiscal and political independence on the world scene. The country's economy is geared to the health and welfare of its population, and there is relatively little outside encroachment. Foreigners can only own property under very restrictive conditions. Nuclear-powered vessels, or ships carrying nuclear arms are not allowed to dock in New Zealand. This seemed a highly evolved sociopolitical attitude, and to me still does.

Next stop Sydney, which reminded me of New York. It had the fast pace, high rises, crowds, museums, and no lack of cultural centers housing music, art, and theater. As seen from a ferry in the harbor, I told Jere that the famous Sydney Opera House reminded me of the gracefully spreading wings of an enormous albatross. He just responded that he wouldn't want it flying over him at the wrong moment. Jere had a limited sense of the poetic. The interior of the symphony hall, within the Opera House complex, is constructed entirely of wood, which lent the vast room a marvelous acoustic quality.

One day, while going up twenty floors in a skyscraper to buy opals, I was accidentally separated from Jere. The elevator doors opened and closed so fast that I had gotten into the elevator car, but Jere, a step behind me, was shut out. Then an odd thing happened. A woman appeared next to me and said, "Don't worry, I'll tell you when to get off." I hadn't said a word, and I could never figure out how she knew that I needed help. To this day, I think that she magically appeared to cure my quandry. Once off the elevator, I found the shop I wanted. It was designed as if it were an opal mine.

The feeling of meeting that woman was only reinforced when I ran into her again later that same day at the Rock, a neighborhood that was restored to resemble historic colonial Sydney. She appeared to me as if by magic twice in one day. Had there been a third time, I might've come out of my reverie and thought that she was stalking us.

As usual, I enjoyed the big city less than Jere, who liked the hustle-bustle of Sydney, while I yearned for the peacefulness of the countryside. As was the case in New Zealand, we had trouble understanding the Australian accent. One day, Jere and I were having a hotel lunch and we were joined by three Australian couples who were traveling together. During lunch, the women and I related to each other, and the men carried on conversation among themselves.

Later on, when Jere and I shared our experiences, I said, "I think women are the same the world over. They talk about their children, their cooking, and clothing. Australian men, as males everywhere, talk about their possessions, their work, and recreation. Maybe it's in the hormones."

"I perked up," Jere told me, "when those Aussie fellows started talking about the 'rice way.' I thought we were in for an agricultural discussion about the rice

136

crop here, and I was primed to compare rice production in California with that in Australia. The conversation became so confused it was like the Mad Hatter's tea party, until I realized that they were talking about a *race* track. So much for that conversation, *mite."*

We traveled north, up the coast to Brisbane. At an animal preserve just outside the city, we saw koalas clinging to tree branches, dazed and drunk on the eucalyptus leaves that comprise their diet. We were told that of the 600 varieties of eucalyptus trees in Australia, koalas will only ingest leaves from a couple of different varieties (And I thought my kids had been fussy eaters). Koalas look playful and cuddly, but they have nasty tempers, sharp claws, and can be quick to defend themselves. We missed seeing the strange duckbilled platypus. They're shy, and only come out of their hiding places once a day to forage for food. We missed one by minutes.

On to Cairns, in the north part of Australia, with its population of rootless aborigines, dispossessed of their land and their economic viability, unhappy, uneducated wards of the state. I talked with a young aboriginal woman, of maybe eighteen or twenty, who seemed absolutely hapless. It was a terrible state of affairs. These people had been almost completely ghettoized and hounded to extinction in Tasmania, the large island just south of Australia. This shameful situation is reminiscent of how we've mistreated Native Americans.

From Cairns, we traveled over sparsely vegetated desert tablelands to the hot, bleak town of Alice Springs at the heart of the island continent. I realized that drought in the outback is so severe and pervasive

as we crossed over dry riverbeds of bleached white stones.

Alice Springs is the gateway to Ayers Rock. It's not mountain nor hill, but a humungous monolithic red rock seven miles around that rises hundreds of feet above the surrounding plains and extends for God knows how far down into the earth. The rock is studded with mysterious caves, reputed to contain the souls of past generations of natives. Those from the legends of "the Dreamtime."

It's a difficult and dangerous climb up to the summit of Ayers Rock. In the store at its base, I bought a little cloth insignia that read, "I didn't climb Ayers Rock." We were only so hardy being seniors, so opted for a bus ride around the rock instead.

The next morning brought a thrilling sight. Jere woke me up earlier than usual and urged me to come outside to see the changing effect of the sun as it rose over the rock. It began as a mysterious black mound over which the sunlight slowly crept. Ayers Rock has silica deposits that cause it to glow from orange, to crimson, to deep purple throughout each day with the changing position of the sun. No wonder aborigines claim that rock has spiritual powers.

Along the road in the outback, we stopped to feed a band of kangaroos that were kept in a large enclosure. There was some kind of grain for sale to feed them, and these big marsupials struck me as mild, friendly creatures, content to hop up to us, enjoy the treats we fed them, then hop away. I wouldn't want to get into a boxing match with one.

It's hard to comprehend how boundless Australia is. It's about the size of the contiguous United States, but appearing more vast due to the sameness of so much of the landscape. Sheep and cattle stations (ranches) are measured not in acres, but in tens or even hundreds of miles.

Unless one has a lot of time and patience, the best way to travel across Australia is by plane. Short hauls are one thing, but the distance across the country is too great with such a monotonous landscape to go by bus. The Australian tourists we'd met in our Sydney hotel restaurant were about to take the last trip on the Afghan Express, one of Australia's famous railroad lines, which was to close down for good.

On to Adelaide, by far my favorite city in Australia. It was festival time, and the city to me was like one great big Greenwich Village. We could see dramatic offerings from dusk till dawn. There was music in the streets, and a happy, carefree atmosphere pervaded everywhere. Adelaide suited my temperament. It was the only city I can think of in all our travels that fit with my particular recklessness. I loved it, Jere didn't. That kind of "hail fellow well met" spirit was just fine with me, but not for my taciturn cowboy.

We visited stockyards near Adelaide, and found to our dismay that the condition of the sheep that had been transported hundreds and hundreds of miles there was shocking. The poor animals were worn out by spending so much time in train car pens with a minimum of feed and water. They came into the stockyards in startlingly bad condition. Jere had an opportunity to talk with local sheepmen about prices of feed and stock. One of them was very kind. He spent quite a bit of time with us and took us out for a meal. He told us that when he'd come to the United States he'd been treated royally, and was only too glad to return the favor. He took us to see a sheep shearing contest and a sheep herding exhibition.

It was a fine end to our three-week stay in Australia. For a New York woman to feel at home around stockyards, sheep shearings, and bone dry river beds may seem unlikely. But to me it was simply a natural progression of my life's events.

A little sadly, we left for Sydney after only a couple of days in Adelaide, then flew home. We had not spent nearly enough time in Australia. It was like having a little nibble of an extremely big cookie.

Farther East Yet—Southeast Asia

As different from each other as we were, Jere and I complemented each other in that his hearing was getting worse and my eyesight was failing. So after some time back in San Francisco and out at the ranch, we thought it was time for a new traveling adventure while we still had most of our faculties.

Our next journey would take us to Hong Kong, the Philippines, Singapore, Malaysia, Thailand, and to Canton in mainland China. This was a circle tour of rice fields, cities, exotic sounds and sights—always alluring, provocative; a wonderful trip, exciting and surprising. For the most part, the people of Southeast Asia are Buddhist, Muslim, or Hindu. We found new, different languages, different ways of dress, a different way of life, and a different way of thinking. Who says that old dogs can't learn new tricks?

Flying from San Francisco to Hong Kong took eighteen hours, with a stopover in Honolulu. We left on a Tuesday and arrived in Hong Kong on Thursday. We had chased the sun halfway around the world and lost a day in the process. That, of course, was because we'd crossed the International Date Line.

The Chung King Palace in Hong Kong wasn't exactly that, but was a fairly decent hotel on the fifth floor of a twelve-story rabbit warren of shops and businesses. I slept for a full day and night. I was so tired after the plane ride that no new sights, sounds, or smells attracted me—only that most welcome bed.

On the ground floor of the Chung King building were shops of all nations and sorts. Clothing shops, clock shops, jewelry shops, sewing machine shops, Chinese crafts, radio and television, music shops, you name it. There must've been more wristwatches on sale in Hong Kong than there are wrists in all the rest of the world. And I always thought that America was such a commercial place. Not in comparison to this city.

The real hallmark of Hong Kong, though, is the teeming populace: the sidewalk crowds that we fought our way through to get to the hotel and the crowds that we crushed into going up elevators. The elevator cars here contained microcosms of the world itself: Indians, Chinese, women in saris, women in jeans, men in pantaloons, men in sarongs, men in slacks and sports jackets. The elevators were built for eight people and generally held at least eighteen. Young Anglo travelers, oldies like us, Indian businessmen, Chinese porters, children visiting with their parents, many of these people carrying packages, carts, bundles, and valises of all sizes, shapes, and nationalities.

On the sidewalks, it was the same thing, maybe worse. We got whooshed along among hundreds of people, so that we began to lose our own individuality in the crowd. We were only two of countless many and just went with the flow.

Some of the most colorful characters are the traveling salesmen from every part of India, Pakistan, and Sri Lanka. Each one carried several pieces of luggage at least the size and weight of each poor little man himself. These wares must have filled their entire hotel rooms. I wouldn't have been surprised if they slept on top of what they hoped to sell.

We watched a Hindu merchant and Chinese merchant sitting on the floor of the Chung King negotiating their business in English, the international language of commerce. Strictly speaking, it was pidgin English (Jere came to call me his little dove because I spoke such good "pigeon" English). The two men were throwing their merchandise—house slippers—back and forth at one another, indicating each of their dissatisfaction with prices, as they jabbered in pidgin English.

In subsequent days, while Jere was writing his serious articles for ranching magazines back home, I had the time to compose some dreadful doggerel.

The salesmen from Nepal and Bombay
Come into Hong Kong, where they stay
To sell belts and blouses and probably trousers
From bursting bags and valises. It must pay.

There was once an Anglo tourist in Hong Kong
Who bought a blouse and a dress and a sarong.
But when she would wear it, no one could bear it
Because she looked terribly wrong-wrong.

(A young Malay woman must be beautiful to wear a sarong and be admired.)

—————

Since I was interested in social welfare and housing, I visited the housing estates for elderly people to

143

see the facilities and conditions in which they live. Jere, on the other hand, being more interested in agriculture, sought out whomever there was in Hong Kong having to do with raising cattle, marketing produce, and imports and exports between Hong Kong and mainland China.

In the high-rise housing estates, I learned that an apartment of 500 square feet was the standard allotment for ten people. The population is too large for more space. I visited one area of the estates that was reserved for the frail elderly in a congregate setting. They shared living quarters, and they had the option of eating in a common dining room or bringing food back to their rooms. I asked the social worker, "What happens when these people quarrel?"

She thought a moment, then answered, "This is hardly ever a problem. We are used to living close together. And we have very large public open spaces."

Mr. Ho, the chief social worker that I spoke to, told me that in denigrating an Anglo, a Chinese is apt to call him a "potato eater," in comparison to "civilized" people who eat rice.

We met a couple of Australians who recommended that we go up to Victoria Peak on the island of Hong Kong. We crossed the bay on the Star Ferry. The harbor was filled with Chinese junks, international steamers, oil cargo ships, and container vessels from everywhere. Four blocks of walking brought us to the cable car railway to Victoria Peak.

From Victoria Peak there is a magnificent bird's-eye view of the city and harbor. On top of the peak we could see how steep and rocky the island is, and why the only way to build is up, up, up. Most of the newer buildings in the central city were between thirty and sixty stories high. We looked down on tall buildings under construction within their bamboo scaffolding. Jere's heart went into his mouth when he saw workers twenty and thirty stories up walking on that flimsy looking scaffolding. From where we were, the structures being built looked like needles poking up from the ground.

After descending Victoria Peak, we stopped in the little town of Stanley for a bite to eat. Laundry was flapping in the breeze. Jere stooped down and picked up a garment that had fallen to the sidewalk from one of the long bamboo arms protruding from windows. "What's this?" he asked me, causing me to wonder which one of us had the vision problem.

"At your age, can't you recognize a brassiere?" I answered. We never found its owner, who obviously was a very tiny woman.

The next day, we traveled to Aberdeen, known for its boat people living on junks, and for its fishing industry. We had lunch, where we were given the choices of crab, lobster, octopus, bass, carp, goldfish, oysters, mussels, abalone, and innumerable other shellfish.

We hired a sampan to take us out into Aberdeen Bay to see the boat people and the fishing fleet. Along the docks, we saw on display newborn chicks, ducklings, and tiny quail, ready to be sold either to be raised or to be eaten at that evening's meal. Some tastes are acquired.

When we returned to shore from our ride among the junks, which looked like ten-foot-high sway-backed workhorses, a couple of boys hopped on the sampan on their way home after a day in school. They were spanking neat and clean in British-style uniforms with school colors on their caps, ties, and jackets, taking the sampan back to their family junk homes. It was a contradiction in lifestyles, a living oxymoron of cross culture.

From Hong Kong, we flew to Manila in the Philippines. We found a nice, pleasant pension downtown, a block or two from the Manila Hilton. It was air-conditioned, with a bar and restaurant, and hot water most of the time.

Jere had been commissioned by a California newspaper to write a few articles on the Philippines. We made an appointment with the head of the Department of Agriculture, who was a young man with a Ph.D. from the University of Texas. We spent a half a day with Domingo Panganeban in his Quezon City headquarters, and learned a great deal about the country's rice culture.

We spent a week in Manila, toured southern Luzon Island, then beat the heat by taking off for the summer capital of Baggio in the highlands.

We stayed in nearby Benawie, the nation's experimental agricultural station where they were attempting to raise cool-weather crops to sell throughout Southeast Asia. It had been suggested that we fly there, but we felt that the best way to learn about a country and its people was to ride local buses. There were always a few people who spoke English, or at least "Tagalish," a combination of English and the native Tagalog.

From Baggio, we went to see the eighth wonder of the world: the rice terraces of northern Luzon. They

146

were built thousands of years ago. Stone walls were built sometimes ten feet high to support twenty-foot-wide rice paddies. The people here planted and harvested rice by hand as they had done for centuries. The little girls took care of the babies while everyone else worked the rice paddies, usually ankle-deep in water.

Stopping for lunch, on the advice of one of our traveling companions, we skipped the most popular dish, chicken eggs, incubated almost to hatching time and plunged into boiling water for a half an hour. Jere and I were up to eating all kinds of unusual food in our travels, but this time we passed.

By the time we got back to hot, humid Manila I was exhausted and got into bed. Jere went out to buy oranges for breakfast. The next morning, he sheepishly recounted his experiences on Manila's jazz strip.

He had settled himself into one of those rock n' roll places, ordered a beer, and a young woman sidled up to him so closely that "the heat melted our clothes." As he expected, the drinks he ordered for both of them cost twice the normal amount, but he was also charged for dancing.

"What's this!?" he demanded. "I didn't dance with her."

He slapped money for the beers only on the table and stalked out. On the way home, however, he realized that he'd left the oranges back at the bar and the stores were now all closed. *If I don't bring oranges back with me, Frances will shoot me,* he thought. So he stormed back to the café, demanding, "Where are my oranges!?" As much as he hated to go back there, he feared my wrath more. Could I really have been such a hellion?

Poor Jere. The least I could do for what he went through was write him a jingle.

> *In Manila it's always a no-no*
> *To make friends with the girls a-la go-go*
> *An innocent beer*
> *Or a masterful leer*
> *Will cost a macho mucho peso.*

Jere's appreciation of the Philippines was now compromised. It was time to move on.

In the multi-cultural city of Singapore, on an island at the tip of the Malaysian Peninsula, we found that nearly everyone spoke our language. Singapore was founded as an English colony by Sir Stanford Raffles. He was a marvelous administrator, setting up an excellent educational system for Malaysia.

Raffles claimed that Singapore would become one of the greatest seaports and trading centers in Southeast Asia. When he purchased the island from the local sultan it was nothing but a tiny fishing village. The sultan told Raffles that he had seen a lion on the island, although there have never been lions there. The name Singapore is derived from sing-a-poora, Indian for lion.

The island is about 300 square miles, a city/state that in the early 1980s had a population of 3,000,000. There were three distinct groups of people living there: Malays, Chinese, and East Indians. The Chinese are the largest group, the other two pretty equally divided, and there is a smattering of just about every other nationality. It is a garden city, and a business, banking, and trade center for all of this part of the

148

world. Rudyard Kipling said that the Raffles Hotel was *the* place to stay in Singapore. The hotel had been kept just like it was when Kipling was there eighty years before. In fact, they still served the same dinner that he feasted on.

The Raffles Hotel bar is a luxurious open-air pavilion with marble floors and walls, surrounded by a garden, with old-fashioned, slow moving ceiling fans rotating overhead. There was an adjacent writing room once used by Kipling, and later by Somerset Maugham. We didn't do any writing there, but did imbibe a gin-based Singapore Sling. This renowned drink was concocted in the 1890s when malaria was epidemic. Gin, quinine, and a few herbs and spices made a pleasant drink that was thought to be a cure-all for mind and body. I took a coaster with the recipe for Singapore slings printed on it, the only souvenir that my son Bill would accept.

To stay at the Raffles would've strained our budget, so we found a more modest hotel in the heart of the Chinese business district, and one block from the famous Bugi Street. In the daytime it's a lovely neighborhood of Chinese shops and restaurants. But by night, all of this disappears and it becomes a transvestite haven, where all the local people gather to gawk at each other and have tourists gawk at them. Pickpockets take full advantage of this mutual curiosity.

The food in Singapore is, in my opinion, the best to be found in this part of the world. It ranges from the inexpensive but excellent fare of Cantonese, Szechuan, and Mandarin street stalls to fine European cuisine in opulent surroundings. We went down Tingling Road, where there's an arcade of shops, each one representing a specific Southeast Asian country. We saw the finest and best-crafted jewelry, cloth, and art objects we'd found anywhere on this trip, displayed in the most artistic and inviting ways imaginable. All in all, it's a most attractive experience for visitors with money. There are lovely things to bring home, though we looked thoroughly and bought nothing.

In some areas of Singapore there are single-family houses for the wealthy. But the key to the dominant lifestyle here—as in Hong Kong—is high-rise housing, also called housing estates. Land is at a premium. An interesting feature of these high-rise estates is that not only do they go up thirty or forty stories and house thousands of people, but the Singapore government intended to build schools, factories, and shopping centers within the estates, so that each one would be a self-contained community. The whole gamut of ethnicities and nationalities in the city living together in harmony and respect in the various estates made a hopeful impression on us during our few days in Singapore. Maybe this would be a model the world over for the future.

The bus system in Singapore left a lot to be desired, with much confusion about the destination of each bus. But in time we calculated how to distinguish wrong directions from right ones. We knew that if we'd figured out the bus system it was time to leave and go up the peninsula to Malaysia.

We left Singapore, impressed not so much by what could be bought there, or by the historical sites, but by the fact that at least three distinct ethnic groups could live side by side in peace. We were also impressed that the buses have plenty of numbers but no names. I came up with the following doggerel:

150

There came a traveler to Singapore
He's on a bus for evermore
He speaks three tongues and maybe more
But he is lost in Singapore.

We took "mystery rides" on those buses, seeing the city but not really knowing where we were going.

The Singapore buses roll hither and yon
But a traveler can't tell which one he's on
You can read the number, you can pay the fare
And you know you're going but you don't know
    where.

We spent fourteen days in Malaysia, which has the same three dominant groups, Malay, Chinese, and Indian. The countries are politically separated, but economically bound together. Most of Singapore's drinking water comes from Malaysia.

We crossed the spine of Malaysia, going from east to west across the long, narrow peninsula that dangles from the underbelly of mainland China like the tail of a kite. The land we traveled was almost all cultivated with rubber and coconut trees.

I was anxious to see Kwanton, which had guesthouses on the beach. I was ever so tired of cities after having spent time in Hong Kong, Manila, and Singapore, and wanted the sweet, quiet relief that only ocean breezes and sandy beaches can give. You could take the girl out of Rockaway, but not Rockaway out of the girl.

It was hot and dusty in Kwanton. We got off the bus and set to work finding a hotel. Our bus driver

151

told a *baychee* driver to take us to a certain hotel in town. A baychee, by the way, is public transportation bicycle built for three, with a driver peddling in front and two seats behind him for his customers. We found that the hotel had a nice foyer, pool, and was generally well appointed, but cost much more money than we wanted to spend—and it was in the heart of town. We wanted to be on the beach.

The women at the front desk (it was women that we were seeing in charge in much of Southeast Asia) suggested a small guest house down at the beach, and kindly got us a taxi. We were taken to the home of a Malay family who had one room for rent. It was small, had no windows, no bath, and a single lazy fan that couldn't stir up much of a breeze. We were wondering whether we should take this accommodation when a young man came in and said, "Come to my house; it's better."

We followed him and came into a small foyer, with a stone floor and steps leading up to a slightly larger room with its own bath, air conditioning, and two beds. It was better by far than what we'd just seen so we took it. But in all our trips, however, it was still just about the worst room we ever had. The sink was falling off the wall, the linen wasn't clean, and we spent the most uncomfortable night, calling to our host for toilet paper. I realized later why there was no toilet paper. The Malays are mostly Moslems, and one is expected to wash after bodily functions without the use of paper.

At the crack of dawn the next morning, we were out, down the road toward the beach, seeking better quarters if we could find them. Greeting us at the ocean's edge was a white sand beach. Beyond our means was the Hyatt Kwanton. But just across the road we found a small hotel—clean, with a large public room and expansive dining room. The people at the front desk weren't Malay, but Chinese. They showed us a satisfactory room for eighteen dollars a night. "Papa," the proprietor, took us in his car to our old dump from the night before, where we picked up our luggage, then drove back and checked into the Kwanton Beach Hotel. This was heaven for the next five days. The hotel overlooked the beach and fresh ocean breezes blew in through our window. The staff spoke English and seemed to enjoy talking with us.

Sitting in the hotel restaurant one morning, we listened to a group of Chinese businessmen conversing in English. As fellow guest and new-found friend, Jacob, a Danish anthropologist, told us that the Malay language doesn't have the technical terms needed in engineering and construction, so English is used.

As for why it took such a circuitous route to find a satisfactory hotel, we learned that in Malaysia the Malays hold the top political posts, Chinese are considered second-class citizens. They are prejudiced against, even though they are the main bankers and moneyed people of the country. No Malay would be likely to recommend a Chinese-run establishment. It was almost the equivalent of a white couple staying in a black hotel in the American South. Indians, though, are at the bottom of the social, economic, and political heap. They're mostly workers on the rubber plantations.

Jacob was preparing for his third trip into the Malaysian jungle. He was studying the changing habits and lifestyle of the Asti Indians, pre-Malay jungle

153

dwellers, and the effects of modern life on their culture. "They're still going about their old ways of hunting and gathering," Jacob told us. "But wherever they go they carry transistor radios."

A few days of relaxation at Kwanton refreshed Jere and me, infused us with new energy, so we hopped on a bus back over the peninsula to Kuala Lumpur, or K.L. as it's called by the locals. Kuala Lumpur means muddy river mouth. The city became Malaysia's capital after the discovery of tin near there, and it remains the center of the country's tin mining industry.

We took a taxi, with our usual hassle over the fare, and arrived at a very pleasant hotel, where we remained for the duration of our stay. Each morning, the bellhop brought us our tea and greeted us most reverently, saying to Jere, "Good morning, grandpapa." He explained that his own grandfather had died a long time before, and he was happy to again call an older gentleman grandpapa. I'm not sure that Jere shared this pleasure, though.

We went to the museum in K.L, which had furnished rooms of the shahs, including a bedroom with diorama depicting the young prince-elect about to be circumcised. Gathered around him were attendants, ministers of the state, physicians, the shah, and a henchman holding an enormous glittering sword. He was a warning to the doctor about to cut the boy that there'd better be no mistake.

There was another diorama showing kite fighting, the manipulation of kites in airborne battle with one another. Another diorama showed giant sea turtles, six to eight feet long, crawling up to the beach to lay their eggs. There is such a problem with the thieving of turtle

154

eggs that the government banned the sale of them. But Jere said that they could be purchased at the outdoor markets.

We took note that a good part of the museum was given over to public education. There was an illustrated civics course emphasizing the value of clean drinking water, healthy diet, preventative medicine, education, family planning, and birth control. I wished that more Americans could see this, dispelling the notion that we alone are so culturally advanced.

We had dinner at a restaurant with a floor show, patronized by the well-to-do locals. It was in a shopping center that would fit into any suburb in the United States. We were seated, getting ready to help ourselves to the buffet, when a Saudi entourage burst in, a couple of dozen strong with loads of children in tow but only three men. The men were in western suits, but most of the women were dressed in their traditional robes, although a few wore western style dresses and had their hair bobbed. Interestingly, the women did not wear veils. The kids looked like teenagers in America, with jeans, T-shirts, and baseball caps worn backward. These people all seemed to be at least trilingual.

They were like locusts at the buffet table. And when they weren't eating they were carrying on at the top of their voices, so we could hardly hear ourselves think. The men sat separately, apart from the din.

The floor show was basically a gamelan orchestra, with percussion instruments played in succession, very much as we would play bells in our country. There were also two stringed instruments similar to guitars. The dances were choreographed in themes of courtship, fishing, and the climate, reflecting indigenous cultural patterns. The hands of the women dancers seemed to flutter as fast as hummingbird wings.

Our last stop in Malaysia was Molucca, the old capital of Malaysia and the center of trade for the East India Trading Company. A city built entirely of red sandstone, Molucca was a Portuguese spice trading center, then the Dutch took it over, only to be displaced by the British, who remained until the end of World War II. But ultimately the Malays persevered and outlasted their conquerers. Today, Molucca is a quiet city. It began as a fishing community and has returned to being that, a rags to riches to rags history in a few hundred years.

Jere wanted to buy a Moluccan walking cane, which turned out to be easier to find in San Francisco than Molucca; similar to being able to buy a Panama hat, not in Panama but in Equador. At the water's edge, beneath high cliffs, we discovered old Chinese burial sites. They were small caves dug into the cliffs with their openings cemented over.

We were taken to a Buddhist temple where we walked through a long corridor leading to a courtyard surrounded by small rooms, each containing a statue of a spirit, in which were burning candles, candles, candles and incense, incense, incense. Judging from the number of candles, some of these rooms apparently honored spirits that were more revered than others. We watched as a woman eased to her knees before one of these statues, touching her forehead to the floor, then effortlessly unfolding herself as she stood up. Her fluid grace in lowering and rising was like the rolling of an ocean wave.

To escape the heat of the low country, we were off by bus to the cold climate of the Cameron Highlands, 5,000 feet up in the mountains. On the way up, I had run out of snacks in my handbag larder, so at a rest stop we bought bananas and delicious crepes, made by a little wizened woman who was probably only about thirty, but looked at least twice that. She dumped creamed corn into her batter, making a crude, lumpy corn crepe, carefully wrapped in yesterday's newspaper.

We took off on the bus for another three hours, climbing higher and higher on an exceedingly curvy road. I was surprised to find myself nauseated and headachy. Jere said that I turned as green as the jungle growth around us. Finally, we arrived in Tapa Rata, cool and clean and plain, a tourist town, not for foreigners but Malaysian vacationers.

We settled into the government guesthouse, similar to the British hill stations of India, a great big Edwardian house with a wide, deep front porch, a large sitting room, and a generous fireplace. We were shown to our suite of rooms with a private sunporch and huge bedroom. On the wall just inside the door was a row of buttons for the lights and ceiling fans. I pushed one, expecting a light to go on. But instead, a young Chinese man, strictly out of P.G. Wodehouse, suddenly appeared at the door, and said to Jere, "You rang, sir?" After he left, Jere arched his eyebrow imperiously at me. "From now on," he said, "you can call me *Sahib* Becker."

We meandered through the town until lunchtime, then went into a Malay restaurant. It had become our habit in Southeast Asia to enjoy varying cuisine daily: East Indian breakfasts, Malaysian lunches, and

Chinese food for dinner. Malaysian restaurants were typically open-fronted, and there we'd have some kind of rice with egg or chicken added to it. On each table was a large copper bowl, and within it a copper pitcher, and on top of the pitcher a cup. They were for use by Muslims, who washed their hands, not so much before each meal as after. Malay Muslims don't use utensils; they eat with their right hands, the left one being reserved for one's private dignity and comfort. It would be an affront for any Muslim to witness anyone eat with his or her left hand. One of the worst punishments a criminal can receive in a Muslim country is to have his right hand cut off, condemned for life to use only his left one.

In the tourist center, we found an ad for trout fishing in the streams around Tapa Rata. It so happened that this area was a popular Malaysian destination for fly fishing. The water is cool and the fish are large and vigorous. Jere was pleased to discover that the rainbow trout around Tapa Rata originally came from the Kern River in California's Sierra Nevada Mountains, where as a boy he'd caught many of this breed of fish.

The time had come to leave the chilly climate of the mountains. We'd been in Malaysia for two weeks and wanted to see other cultures.

On to Thailand.

Thailand extends way down the Malaysian Peninsula, and we rode for hours up the spine of the peninsula through jungles, past rubber and coconut plantations. We were in typical Thai country—rice, vegetables, and gorgeous flowers everywhere. We saw flocks of ducks numbering in the hundreds. When the ducks would land, farmers would frenetically thrash their arms around, sending the pesky birds quickly off their crops and back into the air.

To increase rice production, all the fields had been leveled. But it seemed in every one there was a little mound, perhaps left at the original contour of the land. We figured that these were ancient burial mounds, kept intact by the farmers out of respect for unseen spirits.

In contrast to the bamboo-lathed, plastered, thatch-roofed houses of the Thai countryside, our ride through Bangkok revealed a big, noisy, dusty, and very modern city of high-rises and hot sidewalks. We had chosen the Vien Thia Hotel, which had been highly recommended by our Australian guidebook, *Southeast Asia On a Shoestring*. The hotel promised reduced rates for students. "Why not discounts for us?" I asked Jere. "I'm a student."

"Go for it," he responded. "I'm all for the best damn deal we can get."

So I told the desk clerk when we checked in that I was a student. He didn't bat an eyelash at our age, simply asked to see my student ID.

"Oh, no," I said in exasperation. "I don't have it with me. I left it at home."

Jere leaned over and whispered in my ear, "Show him your blue hospital card. It says 'University of California' on it." That was my sly fox of a lover.

Bangkok is a fairly new city, established on the delta of the Chao Phraya River. Much of the city's transportation is along its klongs (canals). We took a boat on one of them and passed gasoline stations, grocery stores, barges carrying produce and goods to market, and houses whose only entrances were from

159

klongs. All along the klongs, businessmen stood in suits and ties, briefcases in hand, hailing water taxis. Peculiar sights were streetlights placed in the water several feet from shore with electric meters on them. These were read by municipal employees who came along in tiny boats.

There were floating markets in the klongs, where farmers brought their fresh produce and flowers. They would come in skiffs, reminiscent of Venetian gondolas, to sell their crops, and buyers would meet them in their own boats. Nearly all the vendors we saw were women.

Some of the klongs have been filled in. On one of these was the house of Jim Thompson, a former officer in the OSS (predecessor of the CIA) who mysteriously disappeared in the Cameron Highlands in the late 1960s. The architecture and furnishings of Thompson's house were characteristic of wealthy Thai. Maintained by the government, it contains Thompson's collection of ancient artifacts of the highest quality, thoughtfully selected with as great care as what went into William Randolph Hearst's San Simeon. The house had peaked roofs, and the construction was of teak, inside and out. There were lovely small gardens with seating so that one could enjoy the atmosphere and the surrounding greenery.

On the property there was a little spirit house on a pole set in a corner of the garden. These spirit houses we had seen in the front of every residence we passed. Daily offerings of bits of food or flowers were given to the spirit. If he was considered a good spirit his house was set high on a pole; if he was a trickster spirit, though, his house was on the ground.

Whatever there was in Jim Thompson's past was no doubt related to his disappearance. What was left of him was his beautiful home with its exquisite collection, and the silk spinning industry in Thailand, revived at his initiative. Thompson's sponsorship of the old art of Thai silk weaving was his gift to a country he obviously loved.

One of the most important sights in Bangkok is the king's palace and compound. Now, most of the buildings were used as government offices. The architecture was a mish-mash of several different styles, with Italian Renaissance on the first floor, British Victorian on the second, and a traditional Thai peaked roof to top it off. These roofs were made of teak shingles, gaily colored in blues, reds, and greens. The roof trim had enormous wood carvings, painted in gold and other brilliant shades, as intricate as the edging on a French lace handkerchief. The total effect of all this could give one cultural indigestion.

Within the compound were Thai fast food restaurants and a museum with displays of military armor and other historical artifacts. Jere liked having his picture taken with a bevy of teenagers, whom he thought to be the most beautiful girls he'd seen in Southeast Asia. They seemed attracted to him, especially to his broad-brimmed Arizona rancher's hat.

Within the Temple of the Emerald Buddha was the statue of the Buddha, less than two feet high, wearing a robe that the king changes three times a year to represent each season. Thailand allegedly has three seasons: hot/dry, hot/wet, and cool. But anyone who has ever lived in Bangkok for any length of time will say that there are only two seasons. Whatever happened to

161

"cool" remains as much of a mystery as the fate of Jim Thompson.

We traveled north as far as the Mekong River, and looked across into Burma, Cambodia, and the Golden Triangle, where most of the world's heroin is produced. While in the city of Chiang Mai, Jere went to a hothouse to look at orchids. I happened to stay outside and overheard someone speaking English in a familiar American accent. It turned out that person was from California—not just anywhere in California, but Oakdale of all places! Our conversation led to the fact that this man and Jere had heard of each other back home, and they had a mutual friend named Al, from their same area, who'd been living in Bangkok for years.

When we were back in our hotel in Bangkok, we got Al on the phone and he said that we should come right over to his "gold mine" of a bar that supposedly made more money than most gold mines. We were chauffeured over to Al's bar in a limo that he sent.

When we arrived, the first thing Jere asked Al was how he happened to stay in Bangkok.

"I had a bad fall in the construction business," Al said. "I was in the hospital here for a couple of weeks. When I recovered, I had quite a bit of money, and I started to do a little drinking. When I woke up forty-seven days later, I found myself married to this beautiful Thai woman who owned a whorehouse and bar. As husband of the madam, I'm privileged to sleep on the top floor of the whorehouse."

Al's bar was a piece of home halfway around the world, with Americana décor. The posters, pictures on the walls, and newspapers lying around were all

American. "Business is slow tonight," Al told us. "Sometimes you come in here and a guy has just arrived from Saudi Arabia who hasn't had a beer for months, and you can't buy anything because he's treating everybody."

"Do you serve food?" Jere asked.

"Yeah, but I always eat across the street where I can get American food. I've been here seventeen years and can't speak a word of the language or eat a mouthful of the food. I can't even pronounce the name of the street my bar is on. But I have a beautiful wife and a beautiful seven-year-old daughter, and I'm living a very pleasant life."

We ate at Al's favorite restaurant across the street and had a truly memorable meal. The service was impeccable, the table settings reflected the artistry of Thai design in flowers and fruits, and the menu and wine list were marvelous. The luxury of the evening was comparable to the posh Carnelian Room in San Francisco. Here we were two travel bums, falling into a comfort that we sorely needed. Jere, who made his living raising cattle, had scrupulously avoided beef the entire trip because it was so tough. But a steak here was even better than what he was used to back home. Al enjoyed the meal with us, but didn't take a drop of alcohol. I guess his forty-seven day bender changed his ways.

Back in Al's bar, sipping after dinner drinks, we fell into conversation with several colorful characters. There was an Australian cattleman who escaped once a year to Bangkok for his pleasures and always ended up at Al's. (The Actual name of the bar was Lucy's Tiger Den because Al is known there as "Tiger.") There was an international money man, and whatever it was he did, he was raking it in and putting it out into the bottomless pit of Lucy's Tiger Bar. One young man had quit working for the big bucks of Saudi Arabia and was now employed in heavy construction in Israel. Another young man was from Boston, and as he sat with me it seemed that a nostalgia came over him. Just as I was thinking that he might be thinking of his mother, he said to me, "You know, you remind me of Margaret Mead." I didn't think that I looked anything like Margaret Mead, but if I did to him, then so be it.

The next day, we took in the Bangkok weekend market. My eyesight was so bad that I could hardly see the place, but could hear it, smell it, feel it, and taste it. The Thais are a quiet people. Even in this huge, throbbing market there were muted tones of conversation and laughter. The lilting, gentle sounds of the market were lovely and I felt caressed by this atmosphere.

I smelled the spice and incense of the Orient. The market was full of fruits, vegetables, and cooked foods that we'd never experienced before. I touched cloth, artifacts of wood, bamboo, and stone. I touched the faces of children and animals. I touched the wood of the stalls, which was warm and inviting. And the exotic tastes were an adventure all their own.

We hired a *samlor*, a motorized tricycle similar to the baychees we'd ridden. We handed the driver a slip of paper with our destination written on it. But it turned out that our driver couldn't read and was simply taking us to a tourist hotel. We had no way of telling him that we wanted to go in the opposite direction. Jere finally roared at the driver until he stopped the samlor. "I see a man on the sidewalk over there who can read," Jere told me.

164

"How do you know he can read?"

"He's wearing glasses." And Jere was right. The man got the driver turned around and set him in the direction of the Swan Hotel. After a long ride, we arrived, not at the Swan but the famous Oriental, where we diverted our driver around the corner to the lesser known Swan Hotel. The driver jumped up and down like Rumpelstiltskin, demanding a sizeable fee for his circuitous drive. "What shall I do with him?" asked Jere. "He took us on an agonizing tour of noisy, filthy, polluted streets where we didn't want to go, and now he wants to be paid handsomely for it."

"Pay him half of what he wants and that's it," I said. We dispatched the driver and walked back around the corner into the glorious, opulent Oriental Hotel, where we had a drink and watched the changing colors of sunset over the klongs.

We flew back to Hong Kong, and from there to the mainland city of Canton on a four-day visa. We disembarked from the Hong Kong-Canton Railway along with businessmen and their families with radios, TVs, clothing, and who knows what other consumer goods for relatives behind the Red Curtain. Their belongings were carried in the traditional fashion in baskets at the end of poles across their shoulders. Jere pointed out that the baskets were of netted plastic, an incongruous innovation to centuries-old custom.

On the railway platform we met Mr. Wo, who was to be our guide during our stay in Canton. The first thing he said was, "Your president has been shot!" I flashed back to the horror of November 22, 1963, but Mr. Wo assured us that newly elected President

Reagan was being treated in a hospital and was expected to recover in short order.

Our hotel was a surprise, far more luxurious than what we would've chosen on our own. That night I listened with great pleasure to an American film on our TV. It was *I Love You, Alice B. Toklas,* complete with hilarious episodes of characters eating marijuana-laced brownies. I wondered what a movie about pot-eating Americans was doing on communist Chinese television. Perhaps it was meant to denigrate a decadent Western culture.

As a retired rancher, Jere was interested in Chinese agriculture. The two main commodities in the Pearl River delta region are rice and hogs. Jere had grown rice in California, and at one time was one of the biggest hog raisers in the state. The Chinese, Jere believed, were rapidly catching up with the U.S. by importing feed stock and advice from the West.

We returned to Hong Kong by hovercraft on the Pearl River. As we passed ships being loaded and unloaded I thought back on our visit to a commune that Mr. Wo had arranged. The smiling principal had taken Jere and me through his crowded classrooms. I asked if he had naughty children, and if he ever physically disciplined them. "Oh, no!" he answered, shocked at my question. Later, we visited one of the teacher's homes, where we met his wife, who proudly told us about her children's education.

Traveling down the river on our way out of China, I reminisced over a conversation that we'd had with the commune director over a sumptuous midday banquet. Jere had told me later that I had asked so many probing questions that the poor man had sweat on his brow. At the end of our visit, after the commune director's patient responses to everything I'd asked him, I said, "We've asked you so many questions. Don't you have any for us?"

After a thoughtful pause, he queried, "Is it true in your country that you can move about, and live wherever you want, and find a job wherever you want?"

His inquiry hung in the air. All Jere and I could do was simply nod our heads yes. We had learned that those on the commune remained there most or all of their lives.

The plane ride from Hong Kong back to San Francisco lasted a little over eighteen hours. We had crossed over the International Date Line and gained the day that we'd lost when going west at the beginning of our trip. These two oldies were back home after traveling far and wide and adventurously through Southeast Asia on our Social Security—almost.

And the Cowboy Wrote...

When we weren't traveling, which was most often, there were times that I would spend out at Jere's ranch in Oakdale, and other times he would be with me in San Francisco. Then there were times that we'd be apart, he at the ranch, and me in my City-by-the-Bay flat. I was to learn that absence can apparently make the heart grow fonder—if that's measured in frequency of correspondence. During certain periods, my normally laconic rancher would send me so many letters, sometimes almost daily.

The following was written before Jere and I had met face to face. He was already coming on pretty strongly. Callouses on his hands, caked mud on his boots, but quite the romantic.

16 March 1977
Dear Frances:
When I first looked over your resume it frightened me. What, I thought, has this lady (all ladies are women—but not all women are ladies) in common with a guy who was raised next to an Indian reservation and lived his first few years in a homesteader's cabin? And what do I have in common with a brilliant woman who has spent all her life in school, either as a student or a teacher? She has never been more than a furlong from a paved highway in her life. No

wonder she is afraid to come to Modesto for the almond blossom festival, or the peach blossoms, or the wildflowers on display, or daffodil hill.

You told me to put your letters in my bread box... I thought maybe you meant that other kind of bread, and I put them in my safety deposit box (first making a Xerox copy— that's the style nowadays). The Xerox copy I keep under my pillow. However, it does not have the delicate feminine aroma of the original. Should I write to Xerox and complain?

Since tomorrow is St. Patrick's Day, I am enclosing a couple of shamrocks. They are supposed to be descendants of the plants my ancestor 8 or 10 times removed brought over from Ireland when they took him out of prison and shipped him to the colonies and sold him as a bond servant.

It seems that this little note has grown into a real epistle. As one of my instructors at that school founded by John Harvard in 1636 said, "Jere, your reports are just like a babbling brook. They run on and on." But in a dry year even the babbling brook goes dry.
Best Wishes,
Jere

The following letter was sent nine days later, but instead of dating it, Jere wrote:

3rd Day of Spring
Dear Frances:
A few minutes ago I looked up and saw a beautiful rainbow, absolutely marvelous. I instantly ran and jumped into my car to find the pot of gold at the base of the rainbow. But I did not have any luck; no matter how fast I drove, the rainbow moved away even faster. Oh well, with luck like that it is no wonder that I'm still poor.

169

Since reading that you were a delicate flower who need-ed tender loving care I have been carefully studying the sub-ject and I have been forced to change my total thinking.

Before your letter, my favorite character was the home-steader who spanked the heck out of his wife for using his favorite riata (lasso) for a clothesline, instead of putting the clothes on sagebrushes like other wives did.

Anyhow, you have changed my whole way of think-ing—for the better??? Yes??? No???
Regards,
Jere

Five days later, Jere sent me a gag letter that he'd composed. He signed off his cover letter with:

Lovingly yours,
Jere

Frequently, Jere would send crushed flowers in his letters. That was romantic, of course, but it also reflect-ed a man close to the land. I'd uprooted myself from where I grew up, but he was still bound to his place of origin like a tough old mesquite bush.

Thursday, April 7
Dear Diary—This is our secret and must <u>never</u> be revealed.
Tomorrow (Friday) I leave for Modesto. I have finally decided to take a chance and visit that farmer (What is the difference between and farmer and a rancher?) Maybe I will learn. Where is Modesto? I only know that it's in California and only about 100 miles from S.F.
I am hesitant about this trip and this farmer, but I figure

I can easily cope with an old man who was born and raised in a homesteader's shack next to an Indian reservation, and has never been out of the San Joaquin Valley. I am keeping my fingers and toes crossed. The dye is cast. I am crossing the Rubicon.

Friday, April 8
Remember Diary—this is our secret.

I arrived in Modesto on time, but the farmer was not there to meet me. I thought about returning to S.F. but before the next bus for S.F. left, the farmer showed up. Not too good, not too bad. 40 years too old, 40 lbs. overweight, and wearing an Arizona-style cowboy hat with a silver pheasant with feathers in the brim. At least he had bathed and shaved, probably for the first time in a month. I was rather nervous, but then I noticed he was shaking like a leaf, and I said to myself—I can wrap this cowboy around the little finger of my left hand—and Diary, you know I am right-handed.

We finally made it to his ranch, even tho' he was so nervous he could hardly drive—Thank goodness there was no traffic. On the way out, the farmer made some silly statements about almost equal decisions, marriage, etc.—I carefully ignored them.

We finally arrived at his home (such as it is). He had the place cleaned up and put flowers, etc. in my room.

We went out to the local town (Oakdale) for dinner— not too good—not too bad—just passable.

After we returned home, the farmer plied me with Scotch whiskey and inveigled me into his bed, after removing the bundling board he had placed there for his protection. I give him an "E" for effort but an "F" for satisfaction—Oh well, you can't win them all.

The silliest part was when he went out at 5:30 A.M. to

irrigate. In S.F., the ladies of easy virtue are still working the night shift at 5:30 A.M.

I learned the difference between a farmer and a rancher. A rancher can pay his bills and has a little money.

Saturday, April 9
Dear Diary—

Well, I finally got the farmer away from his livestock and irrigation, and after a few cups of coffee we went into town to see the big parade of the year. It was not bad, if you like horses—Oakdale claims it is the cowboy capital of the world.

Back to the ranch and irrigation (how I hate that word) and then into the rodeo—windy and dusty, but no one got hurt, except one clown who got in the way of a bull and got a couple of broken ribs.

Back to the ranch after a N.Y. City traffic jam—the cowboy is not a very aggressive driver—Well, we finally got back to the ranch, and you know what the farmer did, Diary? Yes, he went out to take care of his livestock and irrigate.

Eventually, we drove into Oakdale for dinner—At least the restaurant was well lighted and quiet. He did not invite me into the bar for a cocktail.

About 10:00 P.M., I allowed the cowboy to entice me into his bed. Again, an "E" for effort, and an "F" for satisfaction.

Sunday, April 10

The rancher (I've decided he is a rancher as he always wears boots) got up long before sunrise. Was he going to Easter Sunrise Service? Heck no—He had to irrigate and feed his livestock. "After the livestock, I come first," he says.

We went for a ride thru the Gold Country—the rancher stopped at every historical marker and made me read it. Some markers were interesting.

We stopped at 3 or 4 restaurants before he found one cheap enough in Jamestown (He called it "Jimtown"). What a cheapskate! I guess, Diary, he is a farmer rather than a rancher—Again no liquor, but the dinner was very good, the best yet. But that ain't saying so much.

I again allowed him to entice me into his bed. Not too bad. Third night's the charm.

Monday, April 11

Again, the rancher was up at dawn. At least he had sense enough to leave his work clothes in another room so I could have a morning nap—I think I could train him to be pretty well housebroken, Diary, but it would be an uphill struggle.

We went for another little drive this morning, saw another gold mining town (I guess that is all they have around here) and a bridge built by Gen. Grant before he was recalled by the U.S. Army.

Today I catch the bus in Modesto at 12:10, and back to S.F. I can hardly wait; the solitude is driving me up the wall—The only sound I hear is the thousands of birds singing (mostly at the crack of day)—"18 different species," he says. I guess that proves he can count to 18.

After 4 days of sweating, the cowboy is beginning to smell like a horse—I will have to close now, Dear Diary, as I hear him coming.

Remember, these are our secrets.

If I'd really been keeping a diary, I might have written a few of these impressions of Jere, but certainly not all of them. I believed that a man secure enough in his own identity to poke fun at himself was well worth my time and interest.

I love this one…

Oakdale, Cal
Tuesday,
The 28th Day of Spring
Dear Frances:
I was going to write you a letter, but I did not have any-
thing to say.
Regards,
Jere

…and, of course, this one:

Oakdale, Cal
35th Day of Spring
Dear Frances:
I miss you—
I love you—
I did not sleep a bit well last night—
Love,
Jere

I hadn't experienced such endearment since my lover Jay twenty years before.

Oakdale, Cal
Wednesday—
The 36th Day of Spring
Dear Frances:
I feel very unhappy about last weekend. Looking back-
ward, I find we did not do anything exciting, intriguing, or
educational. I promise that if you are not angry and decide
to come down again, I will try and be a much better host. I

promise I will get the house in a little better shape next time.

I got those big fat hogs butchered today—I was tired of feeding them. The butcher was a day late and a dollar short, as usual.

I had to go to Craig Boss's [one of Jere's grandsons] school's open house last nite—Not too bad—

Otherwise, life goes on at its usual bucolic country pace— I miss you very much—

Jere

P.S. Lovely to hear your voice this morning.

When I took a trip back to New York to see relatives and old friends, Jere's kiddingly paternal words followed me.

Oakdale, Cal
Thursday
The 51st Day of Spring
Dear Little Girl:

Do not allow those Wall St. cowboys to ply you with sweet talk and wine at the same time; take one or the other; not both at the same time.

Don't go outside on a smoggy day, you might be asphyxiated—Don't go on 14th St. After dark. I read it is quite dangerous.

That's all for now. Be a good girl—No fun—but be one anyway.

Love,
Jere

He complained about my occasional admonitions about his dietary practices.

Quit smoking. Quit drinking. No butter. No eggs. No milk. No salt. No cheese. No sugar. No bacon. No fats. No bread—No potatoes—No salad dressing—No pepper. He [any man] does not have to give up sex under that regime— Sex will give him up.

There was more comfort between us and memories to share after Jere and I had been together for about a year.

Friday, 10 Feb. '78
Dear Frances:
I went mushroom hunting today—No luck—A lot came up with the first rains, but at that time we were in Mexico, or was it Guatemala?
It is snowing at Columbia State Park at this time. Remember Columbia? We went there for a Noel Coward play.
The almond trees are starting to bloom; two weeks early—The trees are advertising spring. They are putting out leaflets.
I miss you—
Jere

Being a Social Security recipient didn't keep Jere from writing like a young, illicit lover.

Tues, 28 Feb
Well, Frances Neer, your brother just called to check up on you—I knew you could not get away forever leading a double life. So I told him that you were in San F. I hung up the phone before he could get around to saying he was taking the next plane out here with his trusty double-barreled shot-

*gun to shoot me for besmirching the reputation of his little
sister. His phone call so frightened me that I rushed right out
and cleaned up the mess in the kitchen, even tho' my hands
shook so much that I broke a dish—afraid of that big shot-
gun, but loving you anyway.*
Jere

Far from an ordinary rancher concerned only with
his crops and livestock, Jere noticed every living thing
on—and above—his land.

Dear Frances:
*Since I have nothing else to do, except fold & put away
the wash—wash the sheets & towels, wash the dishes,
defrost the refrig—pick up the papers, feed the livestock, and
irrigate, I thought I would make a list of the wild birds in
and around the yard.*
*A great horned owl—He was raised here as a pet and
released when he could fend for himself—He returned and
harvested about half of the young cottontail rabbits.*
*A barn owl—He lives in the hay barn and catches the
rats and mice.*
*A blue-green skreech owl—He only comes by once in a
while—a very rare bird.*
*The very common billy owls, often called burrowing
owls as they live in holes in the ground—They live on field
mice.*
The large red-tailed hawks.
Sparrow hawks. I once tried to train one for hunting.
The white-bodied kite, quite a rare hawk.
Mallard ducks—They are nesting in the fields.
Blue-winged teal ducks. They too are nesting.
Cinnamon teal ducks.

Crows, of course. They are eating the almonds and screaming at the owls and hawks.

Yellow-billed magpies. They certainly are a noisy bird.

Flickers (a type of woodpecker) They live on ants but love to punch holes in wooden houses.

Red-breasted robins, of course.

And of course swallows—as in Capistrano, Cal.

Chimney swifts—a type of swallow.

Red-winged blackbirds—You noticed them.

The more common Bronson blackbirds.

The yellow-headed blackbirds. They are seldom seen this far north.

Of course there are lots of blue jays.

A few blue birds.

Mockingbirds.

Red-breasted linnets.

A few yellow birds, called wild canaries, but they aren't a true canary.

Once in a while a parakeet someone has released.

California orioles—a beautiful bird.

& 28. Those terrible pests imported from England—the English sparrow & starling.

(Thank God, he spared me naming all the insects.)

Sometimes Jere addressed me with a favorite nickname.

Dear Pancha:

Just a line to let you know I miss you.

Everything is going along at its normal rate. The backhoe got stuck. I thought we would never get it out (we did).

The renter neglected the land so badly I'm having a hell of a time irrigating.

I never drink more than a gallon of wine or smoke more than 5 packs of cigarettes a day.

So you see, everything is normal.

Love,

Jere

Dear Panchita:

Well, another day older and deeper in debt. "I owe my soul to the Bk of Am"—A normal spring day—temp 75— No wind—Birds singing—Young rabbits in the yard. Tom Connolly broke the tractor. A calf fell in the canal and drowned. The back hoe completed his work. Two long days at $22 per hr. A pony broke his stake rope—no harm done.

I'm sorry I forgot to give you the bouquet of roses I had picked for you to take to San F., so I'm enclosing them.

Love,

Jere

Dear Frances:

You are an awful problem to me.

I saw a lot of clothes in the washing machine, so I threw them in with a few of mine and washed everything. When I hung them to dry I noticed they were practically all yours.

Then the state vet's showed up to look at the sheep and I invited them in for coffee and apologized for the looks of the kitchen as I was a widower. They exchanged knowing looks as they had noticed all the female clothes on the line.

You are a problem.

Love,

Jere

Dear Frances:

I haven't anything to write, so won't write anything.

Love,

Jere

P.S.—Boy oh boy, did we have a rain yesterday and last nite. An almond tree blew down across the driveway, leaks in every part of the house (except over my bed), and this morning the canal overflowing into the yard—Never a dull moment—And to think that a couple of days ago I called up the sheep shearer to clip the sheep!

I emptied the bucket that was 1/2 full of water from the Feb rains and it's now 1/2 full again.

P.S. to P.S.—March showers make May flowers—or March rains make May floods.

P.S. to P.S. to P.S.—I saw a beautiful rainbow this after-noon, but I did not follow it to try and find the pot—I already found the pot of gold when I found you.

Jere

Jere's and My Last Adventure

Jere and I became members of Elderhostel tour groups. Elderhostels are one to three-week trips designed for older people. The sites of these tours are commonly university campuses, and the content of the lectures are related to the immediate environment. The experiences that Jere and I had were provocative, challenging, and informative. Good food, good friends, great adventures.

Our first Elderhostel tour was at Humboldt University in Arcata, California to hear lectures on interpersonal relations and make side trips to lumber mills. I was excited to go someplace new and different fairly near home, but Jere didn't want to go up to Humboldt County. After a day or so, I said to him, "Okay, I'm going myself."

"Good."

"Sure you don't want to come along?"

"Hope you have a great time, Pancha."

A couple of days later, though, Jere relented, and for all his criticism of the trip before we even left home, I know it was an eye opener for him.

It felt marvelous to absorb the spirit of California's north coast with its mountains, giant redwoods, and scattered townships. We were delighted by the forested setting of Humboldt State University and the exuberance of our fellow Elderhostel travelers. Dormitory life revived memories of my young college days.

Jere hated the lectures on interpersonal relations (his objection to coming in the first place). He told me that it all sounded like Dear Abby come to life. And he was right, it did. Not so, however, for the lectures on the history of the Northern California coast. Jere feasted on that. For me, the setting and its history were reminiscent of Montauk Point on eastern Long Island, with its whaling history and rugged coastline.

Our second Elderhostel trip took us to study the history, culture, and architecture of medieval England and Wales. We visited three campuses: the University of Sussex, Cambridge University, and the University of Wales in Bangor. A salient memory of English architecture around Sussex were the Tudor houses. Their exposed beams, that we now think of as purely decorative, were the essential tree trunk framework used to build the homes of centuries past.

In Cambridge, we stayed in a house on the central quadrangle of the university campus. There we attended lectures on the humanities and history of the area, and watched students sculling on the river. We didn't take the opportunity to scull ourselves because Jere was not interested in it. But we did a lot of walking and talking and mused our time away in tearooms and pubs.

At the University of Wales, the lecture centered around medieval architecture, science, and the humanities; how the monks lived and learned. One of the instructors got into character, wearing a hooded monk's robe, roped at the waist, with sandals on his feet. He showed us that in ancient days the hand-writ-

182

ten, hand-illustrated, and hand-bound books were chained to tables and desks. They were the precious property of the monasteries.

We took side trips to feudal castles built by the Normans. Canarvan Castle, still enclosed by the original stone walls, had rooms clustered around an atrium, and narrow stairways leading to the upper floors. The stairs were so steep that ropes had been fastened to the walls to assure safety. Even though my sight was failing, I went up and down those dark, steep steps. In lower courtyards I felt the spirit of Sir Walter Scott's *Ivanhoe* envelop me.

Jere and I strayed into many a small teashop for tea and crumpets. One day, from our seat in one such shop, we watched young boys careening down the street on bicycles, their voices blowing in the wind quite unintelligibly. To me the Welsh tongue sounded like a cross between a cough and a gargle. Llanuwchllyn, Clynnogfawr, Rhosllanerchrugog, and Penrhyndeudraeth. I defy anyone but a Welshman to say these words phonetically.

We liked the food in England, as long as we stayed away from English food. Welsh food, at least what was served at the university, was eminently acceptable, and the desserts were divine. The good company we enjoyed made the experience nearly perfect. My favorite souvenirs from Wales were little clay medallions with a red St. George pressed into them. He's the patron saint of Wales.

Our third Elderhostel trip was to Rome. We holed up there at what I called the Convent of the Selfish Sisters. They never gave us enough hot water for showers, we never had second helpings of food, and the whole crowd of us cheered when Jere introduced wine to our un-feasts.

We marveled at the *Thermi Caricola*, with its acres and acres of ancient exercise rooms, massage rooms, steam baths, saunas, swimming pools, and enormous column-bordered quadrangles. The sexes had been separated, men having use of the facilities for part of the week, women having it the other days. As Jere and I gaped at these architectural splendors, we came upon a group of American college students from Arizona. It was their last day in Italy and their last few hours in Rome. I asked one of these students a scholarly question: What had been the most significant experience of her three-week vacation in Italy? Her response: "I'll never eat ravioli out of a can ever again."

We made the obligatory visits to St. Peter's Cathedral, the Sistine Chapel, and the Vatican museums, where my favorite works of art were Michelangelo's *Moses* and *Pieta*, and the *Laacoon*, famous for the depiction of snakes strangling both father and sons. Just as memorable to me was the glowing, burnished all-wood Chapel of St. Theresa. She was renowned for her constant state of ecstacy, allegedly due to the presence of God. But my opinion was that St. Theresa was in a constant state of orgasm. Lucky woman.

We rode the centuries-old Appian Way, mile after mile of cobblestones that linked the world to Rome. My dream of a lifetime turned out to be a narrow, bumpy disappointment, nothing at all like the picture in my high school Latin grammar book. Oh well, all things are not as we would imagine them.

To us, Rome was the height of ancient civilization,

especially in architecture. The Circus Maximus, the Coliseum, the Forum, and the aquaducts represented the glory that was Rome. Our Elderhostel friends went home after two weeks, but Jere and I stayed on and traveled in northern Italy for another two and a half months. We went to Perugia, Florence, Venice, Trieste, and Genoa before returning to Rome.

Midway between Rome and Florence is the city of Perugia, established in the fourteenth century. The physical contour of Perugia is like a corkscrew cut lengthwise down the middle. To get from the bottom to the top of the city, we needed to take a bus or escalator. Down at the bottom, we met a traveler who informed us that the best cup of cappuccino in the whole world was not in Italy, but in San Francisco (And to think we had wasted our time coming all the way here for cappuccino!). Perugia was built on such a steep incline that the escalator had been designed in a switchback course up the hillside to the top. That's where the action was.

Perugia is well known for its chocolate. The city is an open secret, but tourists tend to bypass Perugia in their haste to get to Florence. In so doing, they miss the pleasure of a liesurely population involved in academics and good eating. I was startled by the contrast between the left-wing songs blaring forth in Perugia's town square and the relatively conservative politics of the U.S. I awoke one day to hear a campaign song, fresh and clear in the Italian early morning. *Avanti populi, a la roscosa. Bandiera rosa, Bandiera rosa* (Come on, people, let's go red. Let the red flag triumph) A no-no song in the United States, and a completely acceptable political song in Italy.

On to Florence. *O magnifica Fiorenze!* The city was overcrowded with tourists. We opted to stay in a pension in hopes of escaping the crush. It didn't work. Jere and I walked and walked and walked, visiting the obligatory tourist sights, such as Michelangelo's *David* in the Uffizzi Palace. We were frustrated in the Uffizzi. How could anyone admire works of art when every inch of floor space was taken up by the tortured toes of tired travelers, and every inch of wall space is crowded by horrendous gilt frames overpowering the paintings themselves?

Philip, a friend of mine in the States, having been to Florence the year before, had said to me, "Send my regards to *David.*" By the time Jere and I scrambled through Florence's art, we discovered more than one *David,* and we came upon even more when we got to Venice. When we got back home, we told Philip, "We didn't give our regards to David since we didn't know which one you'd meant."

We criss-crossed the Ponte Vecchio (old bridge) many times. Our favorite quiet place in Florence was the Church of Los Crossos, famous for it Giotto frescos. As often as not, we were the only ones there; we had space and solitude. Once more back on the main drag, we found plenty of places to eat. But unless we veered off to side streets we had to fight for seating.

One of the most famous sights in Florence, indeed in all Italy, is the Duomo, Florence's great Renaissance cathedral, built in the fifteenth century. Two outstanding features of the church were the high arch of the Brunelleschi Dome—the first time this particular technology was used—as well as the bronze doors, cast by Ghiberti in the early 1400s. The original doors were in

186

storage because they were in danger of being worn out by the constant caressing of tourist fingers. But copies of the doors, faithful to the originals, have been put in their place.

We had expected Florence to be a popular tourist attraction, but didn't realize quite how popular. Even the pension was crowded. Too many people at too few tables eating disappointing Italian food. Madame Proprietress, I discovered, was monitoring my every shower. I found later that I was paying for every drop of water I used.

We walked in quiet courtyards and Jere would "read the walls" for me. From the bottom up Jere could tell that a particular building had been started by the Romans, continued by the Crusaders, and finished by the Turks. He could read those walls as clearly as he could the geology of the Grand Canyon.

The most peaceful days we spent in the Florence area were outside the city in the surrounding hill towns. As we stepped off the bus in San Geminino, a walled medieval town, I felt as if I were looking at a picture page out of *Grimm's Fairy Tales*. By bus and by foot, we took in the everyday life of the people. Tortellini was our favorite discovery. These small pasta pockets were filled with basil or meat or cheese, smothered with tomato sauce. *Pax Vobiscum!*

On by rail to Venice, our last stop by train. We two American innocents picked up our bags, walked out of the station, and came to an abrupt halt. Suddenly there were no streets and we could go no farther! We were looking at the canals of Venice. There was water all around us. A kind man asked where we wanted to go. Jere showed him the address. "Oh," said the man.

"Take the *vaporetto* to station six." The vaporetti are water buses, carrying as many as 100 passengers. Disembarking after our ride through the canals, we found our hotel one block away.

Even though Jere and I traveled on the cheap, we had the good luck to find a quiet, reasonably priced hotel in relatively expensive Venice. Our room at the back faced a peaceful canal less traveled. When we ventured forth looking for a meal, we discovered that we were just a short block from St. Mark's Square, with its magestic Campanile, its church famed for its acoustics, and the Bridge of Sighs, linking the church and adjacent prison. The square was teeming with life: citizens, tourists, and thousands and thousands of pigeons.

Once, as we were choosing our destination through the square, we came upon a long line of dispirited tourists schlepping their weary way, eyes glazed, seemingly more interested in the pigeon droppings at their feet than in the splendors around them.

We avoided the tour to the Murano glassmaking factory. I bought a papier-mache mask of Zazi, the city's logo. It was checkerboarded with colored gems, had diamond shapes between the brows and around the eyes, and had a long nose of gold leaf, topped off with a burgandy jewel—a perfect Halloween mask. I also bought a gondolier's flat, straw hat. I'd intended to give both to Christine, but kept them for myself. She could come over to my place and enjoy them, and I knew that Bill would enjoy their whimsy as well.

We found out that Venice is not all water, and we walked through back streets over dozens of little arched bridges. The facades of the houses showed the centuries-old water level in the city. The front walls of the buildings looked like they were hardly connected to the streets on which they stood. Even the ground level of the palaces on the canals showed where flood waters had risen and fallen over centuries. The change in water levels left shabby looking discolorations in the fronts of buildings, part of the dissipated charm of Venice.

Jere and I avoided the de rigueur rides in gondolas, being most comfortable taking the vaporetti. We went to see the paintings of Tintoretto, a Renaissance artist who worked almost exclusively in Venice. It was too bad that my sight was dimming and I couldn't fully enjoy the dramatic colors, especially the reds. Although I had the same disadvantage in Peggy Guggenheim's Museum of Modern Art, at least the light was brighter there, and the paintings hung sufficiently far apart so that I wasn't faced with hardly any light in an old church.

In the week we were in Venice we returned again and again to Station 29 on the vaporetti. No other travelers seemed to know about the district. It had a good café where wine flowed freely and our favorite dish was steamed periwinkles (tiny snails) in olive oil. Oh, glory! I brought back a bag full of those tiny periwinkle shells for Christine.

When we checked out of our hotel, we said to the manager, "We really don't know why we're leaving."

"You'll be back," he told us.

And so we bade farewell to the most salubrious of cities, the most wonderful of climates. We rode the vaporetto one last time to the railroad station, and boarded the train for Trieste, the port at the north end of the Adriatic Sea.

The intentional high point of our trip to Trieste was to see the stunning Dalmation Coast in Yugoslavia. We tried to visit this country, but our taxi driver misunderstood our request to take us to the visa office and drove us instead to the border, where we were turned away. The next day, we managed to get visas, but couldn't get train or bus tickets into Yugoslavia. A visit to Yugoslavia for us just wasn't meant to be, so we gave up and headed west.

We rode the rails, bypassing Padua, Bologna, and Milan until we got to Genoa. We stayed there for a couple of days before returning to Rome. Genoa is beautifully situated on steep hills overlooking the Mediterranean. Jere and I took a bus tour to get an overview of the city. One thing I knew about Genoa was that Marco Polo was thrown into prison there for passing the first bad check ever written. No bank was about to accept a piece of paper in lieu of cold hard cash. Nevertheless, Polo ended up settling in Genoa after his travels to China. He had brought back with him those little strings of dough that the Italians came to call spaghetti.

Jere said that the Italian Renaissance was vigorous because the artists of the period had the strength to hammer and chisel marble and lie on scaffolding to paint the ceiling of the Sistine Chapel. They had plenty of wine and pasta to keep themselves hale and hardy. Jere theorized that the Renaissance England experienced at around the same time was developed by playwrights and poets, huddled and scribbling away in dingy garrets because they only had beer and fish & chips for sustenance—brain food instead of brawn food.

Our last stop before returning to Rome was at Ostia Antica, a long-abandoned settlement on the Tiber River near Rome. In its own way, Ostia Antica gave us the same feeling as did Pompeii and Herculaneum, farther south close to Naples.

Back in Rome, we returned to the Hotel Souvenir, set on one of the city's seven hills. We had come to the end of our three-month pilgrimage through northern Italy. We settled in just long enough to enjoy the quiet of the hotel's lovely garden and the local sidewalk cafes for wine, cappucino, and Italian delicatessen before flying back to New York on Alitalia. I had plenty of legroom, but unfortunately a set of twins stepped all over my legs going back and forth from their seats the entire way across the Atlantic. Jere had slightly less legroom, but more peace.

My niece and nephew, Luisita and Bert, met us at Kennedy Airport, took us to Chinatown for dinner, then back to their house on the Upper West Side. We spent two nights with them, then back to the airport for our flight to San Francisco. There was a delay at Kennedy that lasted for hours, not quite long enough for an overnight at the airline's expense, but long enough to get complimentary meals. As I sat in the noisy, crowded waiting room, I felt a premonition, as if something terrible was about to happen. I feared the obvious, that our plane was going to drop out of the sky while crossing over the Mississippi River, but that didn't happen. The flight went fine, even though I still sensed some ominous cloud on the horizon.

Bill didn't meet us at the airport as we'd expected. His friend did. As we were about to get into his car, he said, "Bill is sick. He has AIDS."

191

Crisis, Tragedy, and a Second Chance

We just stood there in shock at the terrible news. Through my own tears I saw Jere take his handkerchief and dab at his eyes. He and Bill had been firm friends with great practical understandings in the business world about what ranching and real estate had in common. They had grown to like and admire each other very much.

My life, and Jere's and my life together would be forever changed.

Until he died three months later, I spent every day with Bill. We ate together, laughed together, reminisced, arranged business matters, and set our house in order. His wife Ann was also quite ill from complications of diabetes, and would pass away herself about a year and a half later. Bill presented me with a challenge. "You as an old person will have to bring up a young person." He and I agreed that I would move into his home to take care of thirteen-year-old Christine.

My being "old" was less of a problem than the fact that I could no longer see. Bill, lying on the couch, would read me the newspaper, book reviews, and articles from psychology journals. His phone was constantly ringing. Many of the calls were from well-wishers, and others were asking his advice about everything under the sun. Until his last days, I never realized his force in the community. Even now, almost twenty years later, people remember him for his good fellowship and wise counsel.

Bill had decided to renovate his flat, but I told him it was too big a project. He said, "I'm going to start it anyway." The renovation turned out to be so extensive that I would have to finish it myself after Bill died. In his wisdom, he knew that challenge would help sustain me.

Bill passed just short of his forty-sixth birthday. He was the apple of my eye and the core of my heart. We spent those last months of his life celebrating sweetnesses and laughing at ridiculous jokes. One of our favorites was one that Henny Youngman told about his wife.

"Oh, Henny, I was in Macy's today, and bought the escalator."

"Impossible. How could you do such a thing?"

"It was marked down."

Bill had prepared his memorial. More than 200 people attended, and whoever wanted to get up and talk took the podium and spoke about the Bill they knew. One man said that Bill had been the best friend he'd ever had. One of Bill's business associates said that Bill was the only one on his board of directors who he could trust. Still another person said that Bill's judgment was impeccable.

I stood at the podium and said that Bill's book of life was short but closely written. I spoke for Bill when I told of his three bequests. To Christine: that she use her time wisely and profitably, and that she use her gifts of art and music for her benefit and the benefit of others. To his friends: that they enjoy the days of their work and the days of their pleasures. To me, Bill left a bouquet of friends.

193

There was no time to mourn. I needed to rally my strength and take care of Christine, to bring up a teenager whose father had just died and whose mother was terminally ill. My daughter Amy, living across the country, said to me, "Even in our deep mourning, how lucky you are, Mom, to have a second chance to bring up a thirteen-year-old girl." I was to become Christine's de facto mother, which made me reflect what motherhood meant to me. I never related that closely to my own mother, so never was sure what the role was supposed to be, was never comfortable with the idea of "raising" a child. So I thought more in terms of living with Christine as her granny and guide.

Jere was also living with us. He wasn't going back to the ranch as often as he did when he and I were staying in my little apartment. His health was failing.

We hired a housekeeper to do the marketing and cleaning. Christine would cook (her meals were delicious) and I would do the cleaning up. She had no mercy on me when it came to the number of pots she used. Like as not, she'd throw eggshells across the kitchen into the sink, knowing that she had no cleanup responsibilities.

Although I hated getting up at 7:00 every school day morning, I couldn't bear the thought of Christine starting the day alone. Breakfast was our favorite quiet time together. Part of the fun was listening to music and guessing who the composer was. Afternoons were reserved for homework and gossiping over what had happened at school. Christine had a chance to talk about which teachers she enjoyed and the shenanigans of her friends.

Some of our best times together were when

Christine did her high school homework. I learned a lot of chemistry from her. I learned some Spanish also, augmenting the little I'd picked up from Jere in our travels. Helping her with her homework was something else again. I could no longer read. Whatever problems Christine had in her homework she needed to read aloud to me. One day, she said, "Granny, I need help with my algebra." My heart sank. I hadn't been that good in algebra myself, and now I couldn't even read the problem. I asked her to read it to me, so she did, and together we figured out the procedure for solving the problem. Then we looked in the back of her textbook and discovered we had the wrong answer. We repeated the procedure, Christine reading the problem a second time. We checked the answer and found we were wrong again. We did the procedure a third time. "Okay," I said to Christine, "read it aloud again and let's see what we missed."

"Granny," Christine said halfway through, "I kept leaving out a parenthesis." We redid the problem, this time including the forgotten parenthesis, and—oh, glory—we got the right answer!

Another time, Christine told me she had to read Keats' "Ode to a Grecian Urn."

"I hate poetry," I told her.

"So do I."

I asked her to read the poem aloud, which she did. "What does it mean?" I asked after she'd finished.

"I don't know."

"I don't know, either," I said. "Let's read it again."

This we did several times, until the images of girls and boys on the urn finally started to come to life for us, and what these teenagers were doing—pursuing each other in romantic desire—took on significance. In her final rereading, the beauty of the language and its rhythm gave us pause, and we began to understand the picture on that Grecian urn—"Beauty is truth and truth is beauty." We agreed that it was a lovely poem and that maybe neither one of us hated poetry after all.

All was not harmony, however. Exacerbating our living arrangement was the fact of Jere being there too. He was in poor health, growing weaker with age and too much cigarette smoking over the years. He was more and more grumpy. And he and Christine were vying for my attention; each one wanted all of me. Jere and Christine stopped talking to each other and I became a go-between.

I called my friend Dr. Kenneth Pelletier. We spent an hour on the phone. His considered opinion, as a psychiatrist and humanist, was that the three of us were a family, albeit a strange one. "You cannot be a switchboard," he told me. "Have a meeting with Christine and Jere and explain this to them. What you have to say to each other, you need to say directly." We were uncomfortable, but did the best we could.

One evening, Christine rushed into the bedroom. "Granny! Jere's on the kitchen floor! He's not moving, but still breathing." I helped Jere to his feet and to the couch. After he was feeling better he said that he'd had a heart attack. I wasn't so sure about that, but advised him to see a doctor. I looked at him for a long moment and added, "I think it's time for you to go back to the ranch and let Inez take care of you." I was nearly blind and couldn't do a good job of it anymore. So Jere did return to the ranch. He passed away seven weeks later.

196

As sad as Jere's death was, the pall was lifted from Christine and me. Jere and I had had nearly a decade together. Most of it was mutually enriching. I missed him, certainly, but my life had taken a new course. Christine was now my priority. Maybe I could be more of a help to her growing up than I had been to either Bill or Amy. When they were children, my energy had gone into pursuing my own career as a teacher. Marriage, housekeeping, child-rearing were secondary to my personal drive. Quality time with my children had not been in my vocabulary. When Bill died I was in the middle of working on a masters degree in low-vision studies. Even though I had lost my sight, I still was drawn by a thirst for academic knowledge. But now I had a new career that took precedence: to give my primary energy to Christine, to make life comfortable for both of us.

Our new life began, and Christine and I became more lighthearted. The house was filled with Christine's friends, my friends, our friends. But Christine and I also had our private sadnesses. I knew that when she retreated to her room to draw or listen to music, or came out into the kitchen to bake chocolate chip cookies, that her heart was heavy with the loss of her parents. There was a hole in her life and in mine that we could never fill. All we could do was try and make that emptiness more bearable.

And I had to be tolerant with Christine—up to a point. I soon found that I was losing control of the social situation because well-wishers who'd been close to Bill were inviting Christine on activities without consulting me. I had to control these people in order that they not take control of Christine's life. I told

197

them, "I represent Bill now, and as you would've consulted him, you now needed to consult me."

With some reluctance they said, "Okay, Frances." But it wasn't long before this exchange was apparently forgotten.

One day, I finally called a meeting of Bill's friends who were involved with our family so that I could spell this out loud and clear. I explained that Christine needed peace and quiet, she had school to attend and homework to do, and she couldn't just be going off on overnight trips or other social engagements at the drop of a hat. I made it clear that I had promised Bill that Christine's welfare would be paramount in my life. Looking back now, I wonder if there wasn't that old specter of me once again being alone in a crowd, that I felt somehow left out by Bill's friends paying so much attention to Christine. That could have been an element, but I still knew that the well-wishers needed to ease off with their solicitous behavior toward Christine. And they came to see things my way.

That wasn't always the case with Christine, though. She had a whim of iron, so we had our share of conflicts. In our first days of living together, Bill's friend Emmett would call me every morning as Bill had done. Each morning, Bill would call and say, "Hello, Mom, how are you? I'm busy, can't talk very much. So long." Emmett picked up from Bill, and for many weeks he called to say, "Good morning, Frances." And I would take the opportunity to complain to him about what Christine was and wasn't doing, what she should and should not be doing. Wise Emmett, who was a therapist, finally said to me one day, "Frances, let go of the rope." With that sage advice, I started to understand my path toward a healthy life for Christine and me. I had to "let go of the rope," but be ready to grab hold of it when Christine needed boundaries.

One friend offered to teach her to drive. Another bought a ticket for her to a rock concert. And other friends were anxious to take Christine to symphonies during the school week. When I thought that their attentions interfered with Christine's studies, I fended them off. Christine didn't understand why and what the dynamics of the situation were. Her retribution to me in those days was that she would blame me for whatever negative was happening. I knew that I would not answer her nor call her to task because she needed to get her resentments toward me out of her system.

By the time she was sixteen she had learned to drive, had a license, and was staying out later than I wanted her to. And there was no way of telling her to shape up (I said she was willful). So, one day I told her, "The car is grounded."

She said back defiantly, "But *I* have the keys." Clever girl, my granddaughter.

Another time, I had gone out to a meeting. When I came home Christine wasn't there. I knew where she was. And she stayed away for nearly a week. She was just up the block and around the corner. I spoke to the mother of Christine's friend, where she was staying. By the end of about five days, I asked Christine to please come home, and so she did. But during the week she stayed away, instead of cajoling, or blaming, or crying, I just let it ride. None of those reactions would've done any good anyway. Christine said to me at one point that she was glad she didn't have a father or mother because so many of her friends were having trouble with their parents and at least she didn't have that problem.

Our best times at home were when Christine read poetry, short stories, books, and articles in newspapers and magazines to me. She took the time to describe pictures to me. After all, she was a budding artist and I was a granny who couldn't see any of the work she did or any of the pictures that she found so enjoyable. And we listened to a great deal of serious music, guessing who the composers were and what kind of orchestrations were being used.

In one year, Jere died, Christine's grandfather died, her mother died, and my brother Harry died. It got so that Christine would come home from school and say, "Well... who died today?" But the house had good vibes. And it wasn't empty; it was full of people, visitors and live-ins. Christine's cousin Christopher came to stay for about a year. They were good friends. Then there was a young man named John who was a live-in, helping with housekeeping, marketing, and cooking. And so the three young people were good companions. When Bill and Amy were kids and having an argument, if I got in the middle of it they would gang up on me. That's what happened in this house. Even though I was paying the bills, the three of them had their own secret society, and if necessary would oppose me. That was alright, even healthy, as far as I was concerned.

Christine went off to college, far away from me as I'm sure she needed to be, up north to Evergreen State College in Washington. She paid close attention to her studies, and since most of her classes were seminars, she assumed responsibility for her own preparation.

At her graduation, just a few seniors were recognized for their community involvement. Christine was one of them. What more could I ask? She was a serious, responsible student, fulfilling Bill's bequest to her, using her time wisely and profitably. She had a good social outlook. It was natural for her to be a volunteer worker at the Lighthouse for the Blind in San Francisco because she had been living with a grandmother who was visually impaired. Christine well knew that physical differences needed to be understood and respected, not disregarded.

My purpose in our years of living together was to accept Christine for who she was and help her build on her strengths. She loved drawing, music, cooking, and baking. She loved sports, and she always took her schoolwork seriously. I only hope that she ultimately saw me as her champion, for that was always my intention.

When Christine was in college, Bill's friend Ron said to me, "I thought this was a lose-lose situation. I never believed it could work. But the two of you have done it." To this day, Christine and I love, respect, and celebrate each other.

In guiding Christine through her adolescent years, I'd always tried to heed Bill's advice. "Enjoy the days of work, and savor the days of pleasure." Whatever strife Christine and I went through together, what stays with me so resoundingly about living with her was the enjoyment and pleasure we shared. And what I've come to feel is immeasurable pride in the bright, passionate, generous-hearted young woman she is.

Moving On

Christine's and my relationship, with a few bumpy exchanges every so often, had managed to develop nicely during her teen years. She was growing in all the right ways, and with less and less to do in terms of guiding her, I found myself needing renewed purpose. I realized that I should focus on what was important in my life now, to marshal what forces I had left to do work that would give me some measure of personal happiness and excite my passion.

In the preceding few years, the course of my life had been dictated by crises: Bill's death, Ann's death, Christine's grandpa's death, and the sudden need for me to raise Christine. Blindness was more of an obstacle than a crisis. I couldn't afford to let my impairment be an overwhelming loss since that would interfere with Christine's needs. But blind I'd finally become in the swirl of events, and I would be downplaying it unrealistically if I regarded my loss of sight as anything less than traumatic. For better or worse, life changes with conflict. How we deal with whatever conflict we have defines our maturity. That, in turn, is shaped by our self-enabling conditions. What we understand of our own resources and how we utilize them outlines our success. No matter what our disability might be, our success in life is a matter of what we can do in the face of conflict, in meeting the challenges of physical, mental, and/or emotional hardship. I could either be mensch enough to myself to live to my fullest, or just wimp out.

I'd known for years that blindness was just outside the door of my existence, waiting to enter. When it did, I couldn't just drive it away. I had essentially three choices: bemoan my sightlessness ad nauseum, deny it (hard to do when I was bumping into furniture all over the place), or... embrace it somehow. If being blind was now part of the definition of who I was, then I needed to find out more about that facet of myself.

While I still had been with Jere, I'd started to develop a low vision group that eventually turned into the Visually Impaired Persons (VIP) Forum. I had also gone back to school to earn a masters degree. Blindness may have become my burden; I also took it on as my focus of interest.

Other low vision students in my classes had a common complaint that their ophthalmologists were not paying enough attention to them. This caused me to speak up to my own doctor. "Michael, too many of you are treating patients as 'eyes,' not as people." As soon as I blurted that out, he got a phone call from another one of his patients. I listened to the quality of his remarks. After he hung up, I said, "That's just what I mean. You gave that person on the phone the brush-off." To his credit, Michael stepped down from the lofty pantheon of physicians to consider what I'd told him. He encouraged me to write recommendations that could facilitate well-being for the visually impaired, and I came up with three basic concepts:

1. Physicians need to regard patients as people, not underfunctioning "eyes."

2. Technicians in the eye clinic should be informed about the day-to-day problems that confront low-visioned people and should be prepared to make community referrals.

3. Develop community education for family and friends, as well as for the vision impaired themselves.

These guidelines could not have come to fruition without the sponsorship of the Department of Ophthalmology of the University of California Medical Center. My recommendations got the blessings of Dr. Stephen Kramer, chairman of the department. He also helped me write a guidebook for the visually impaired, *What's in San Francisco for Us?*

During that time, I also became involved in a low vision "support group," a term in increasingly common usage. But the word *support* to me brings to mind girdles and garters. I preferred to think of us as an affinity group. The young man who organized the group's activities had a degree in public health, but he relied on me for my ideas. After awhile, I realized that A) He didn't seem to have much in the way of his own ideas, and B) He was getting paid and I wasn't. I decided not to be cooperative anymore. I wasn't here to prop him up. The poor fellow seemed puzzled when I stopped like a stubborn donkey from offering any more suggestions in group discussions.

One of the few male clients who came to these meetings was a tall, handsome Irishman named Jim Riley. He had been blind for about fifty years. I soon began to notice that if I came to a meeting after Jim had arrived, he got up from wherever he'd been sitting and walked over to sit next to me.

Thus began a romance that lasted a decade.

Jim had a wonderful sense of humor. During the meetings he and I would one-up each other and entertain everyone else with jokes. I'd always heard that Jews and the Irish get along well; much of what they have in common must be their great capacity of finding amusement in the human condition.

Jim was my senior by a bunch of years, but he reassured me that he'd be around for awhile. "I may be eighty-eight, but don't worry, I have older brothers who are just coming into their prime.... How old are you?" he asked me.

"Seventy-one."

"No, you're not. You're seventeen."

Jim kissed the Blarney Stone way before he ever kissed me.

While Jere's and my time together was characterized by travel to exotic places, Jim and I rarely left San Francisco. But within the City we did get around. And both of us being blind, there was a sharing of fearless adventure. Jim had been a gambler of long standing, so he was used to taking chances, and I wasn't one to just settle for a sedentary life. We negotiated our way down unfamiliar streets. There was so much to smell and hear out there—and to taste, of course. For several years, Jim and I were quite the restaurant hoppers. We particularly liked Harrington's in the Civic Center. When the bartender saw us coming he automatically set up two Irish whiskeys. And there was a sidewalk café, the name of which escapes me, that had the most tender and delicious lamb chops. Waiters and cab drivers were friendly with us. I'm sure it helped that we were uncommonly sociable with them.

One of our favorite cabbies, Ed Matthews, picked us up one morning at my house. "I knew there was something going on," Ed said. "Jim was wearing the same clothes as he had on the day before when I picked him up to bring him here."

One day we hired a cab driver who knew us well. He took us to the Mission District and described in vivid detail the street murals there. We were amused at his depiction of a woman who "walked into a mural." The door to her apartment building had been painted as part of the mural, so she entered the huge design. What a marvelous concept! That cabbie did an exemplary job of being Jim's and my eyes that day.

We made brief sojourns, about an hour's bus drive north of San Franciso, to visit his daughter, who had four delightful children.

Another adventure was flying down to San Diego. My daughter Amy and her husband Bruce were coming out from the East Coast to be there to attend a professional conference. So I availed myself of the opportunity to see them while they were in California. Also, it would give me a chance to visit my friend Herbie who lived in San Diego. He had been the best man at my wedding.

Amy knew with whom I'd be staying, but didn't have the number. She called every Herbie Solomon in the San Diego phone book until she tracked us down.

Herbie, Jim, and I went the few miles across the Mexican border to Tijuana one day. I found a purse there I wanted to buy and, as was the custom south of the border, negotiated fiercely on price. Before, in Latin

American countries, Jere had done all negotiating, being fluent in the native language. On my own, I did as well as I could with a smattering of pidgin Spanish (a.k.a. "Spanglish"). It must've been hard for the vendor to take me seriously, however, since Herbie just about fell over laughing at how I was fracturing this foreign tongue.

While in San Diego, I called my second cousin Richard Lief, son of the man who'd officiated at Joe's and my wedding. I'd never met him, but we felt immediately comfortable with each other over the phone, swapping jokes like old pals. After cracking up at one of my better punch lines, Richard said, "It's no doubt, Frances, that you're a Lief."

Our farthest adventure took Jim and I to Nashville, Tennessee for the marriage of his grandson. "Grandpa, you walk down the aisle with Frances," the groom insisted. I found it quite open-minded and endearing that he wanted his grandfather to walk down the aisle with his mistress.

For about five years during this time, I co-hosted a radio cooking show, "Of Cabbages and Kings," with John and Lynette Evans. We interviewed Bay Area restaurateurs and chefs. When Narsai David, a local cuisine maven and restaurant owner, was on our show he happened to say that a certain recipe called for kosher salt. To which John popped in confidently with, "There is no such thing."

I spoke up before Narsai had a chance. "John, you've heard the story about Sodom and Gomorrah?"

"You mean from the Bible?"

"The very same."

"Of course. The wicked cities and all the wicked

people in them were destroyed. The one just man, Lot, and his family were spared. What does that have to do with kosher salt?"

"Remember what happened to Lot's wife?" I asked.

"Against God's orders, she looked back at the burning cities."

"And..?"

"And she turned into a pillar of salt."

"John," I said, "Lot's wife was a Jewish woman. Now what sort of salt do you suppose she would've turned into?"

While co-hosting "Of Cabbages and Kings," I met another man with whom I was to have many wonderful times. I had heard him hosting his classic radio show, "The Music World of Joe Thompson." Old memories flooded back over me when he played two hours of Paul Robeson's recordings. Joe also intrigued me when, in speaking to his listening audience, he complained of a recent cloudiness of vision. Being familiar with the basic causes of visual impairment, it sounded to me as if Joe Thompson had some eye problem. I called him at the radio station to find out how I could help him. It turned out he needed encouragement to get his cataracts removed. Thus began a beautiful relationship, totally platonic, which lasted several years. Joe was a true Sybarite, who indulged in the finest of wines, haute cuisine, good music, and the latest in theater. Being in his company meant evenings out on the town in high style.

Jim liked to dine out, but his taste buds weren't nearly as sophisticated as Joe Thompson's. Once when dining at Masa's, possibly the most exclusive restaurant in San Francisco, Joe asked what side dishes came with his order.

"Moroccan rice," the waiter replied. "With currants and native herbs."

I gazed haughtily up at the waiter and said, "Mr. Thompson prefers spuds." Joe looked askance at me, smirked a little, and went along with the joke.

Our waiter was a bit taken aback. "I'm sorry, madam. What was that?"

"He'd like spuds instead of the rice."

"I'm not at all sure—"

"He's allergic to rice. Goes into convulsions at the first bite."

"Oh, I see," said the waiter, relieved at some explanation.

"You wouldn't want that to happen, would you?"

"Certainly not, madam. I'm sure we can make some substitution."

"And that would be spuds."

"Spuds... I'll see what we can do."

Joe got spuds (once someone in the kitchen determined that was just potatoes). The only thing is, as Joe told me later, he would've preferred the Moroccan rice.

Christine was concerned about my nighttime drives with Joe Thomson, as he had a tendency to drink to excess. "Granny, don't drive with him," she warned. But I continued to do so.

One night, after a cop had stopped him for speeding kitty-corner through a parking lot, I said to him, "Take it easy, Joe! It's too late for me to die young, but at least I want to die in bed."

Joe knew all the movers and shakers in the music world. And he was a big spender. His financial advisor had warned him that he'd better quit wining and dining so much or he'd eventually go broke. Once I tried to influence him toward a more calm, ordered lifestyle. "Joe, you must stop your profligate ways, or else you'll have to come live in my guest suite."

I expected him to thank me, but instead he said, "Do you have a phone down there?"

After I'd known him for about eight years, Joe Thompson passed on. I wasn't with him at the very end, but I'll bet he left this mortal coil with a smile on his face. What a character.

There was another man who I came to know well through my low vision work. My relationship with Jack Kaufman was also strictly platonic. I met him through the VIP Forum. He had presented me with a sheepskin proclamation in appreciation for my having instituted the Forum. He was a fellow with quite a flair for the dramatic, who gave the best recitation of Robert Service's poem, "Dangerous Dan McGrew" that I've ever heard.

Jack and I tested walking routes in Golden Gate Park for the vision impaired. Among several other places, we found a grove of fig trees, good for secluded picnics, and a more public picnic area near the park's magnificent huge greenhouse, The Conservatory of Flowers.

Whenever I was mad at Jim Riley, Jack Kaufman and I went dancing. He was a wonderful dancer, leading with such grace and assurance that I almost felt like Ginger Rogers. When I thawed from my anger at Jim and wanted to make up with him, I needed to stop going out dancing with Jack. Once, for an excuse, I feigned injury, showing Jack the Ace bandage I'd

no strong sexual relationships in her life except Christine all men/female

wrapped around my leg. His response was to hike up his pant legs. "Hell, Frances, look at me." Jack had Ace bandages on both of his legs.

When Joe Thompson took me out, he'd typically bring me a box of candy and a bouquet of flowers. Jack, on the other hand, would bring a modest African violet plant. While less showy, this gift touched me more. I've always loved the understated beauty of African violets.

As with Joe Thompson, Jack Kaufman frequently took me out to dinner and the theater. His hearing was failing, along with his eyesight, and the last time we went to a play, Jack left me sitting in our reserved seats to go off and search out a place where the acoustics were better. In his frustration at the loss of two of his senses, Jack would lament to me, "I'm falling apart."

Even with the gastronomical and theatrical delights I had with Joe Thompson and Jack Kaufman, the man in my life during these years was still Jim Riley. Being tall, handsome, and witty, there was little I had to complain about Jim, except for his occasional displays of bad temper and his increasing inclination toward apparent narcolepsy.

"Go home and sleep in your own bed, Jim," I finally told him.

"Whadaya mean? Why?"

"Because you fall asleep with me as soon as your head hits the pillow."

"Well, I'm ninety-six years old. Whadaya expect?"

"If I'm seventeen, as you've said, I expect my guy to be at least conscious for a little while when we go to bed."

"Aw, Frances..."

"You're of no use to me. Go on home."

And he did for the last two years of his life, although we talked on the phone, usually many times every day.

I had shared nearly a decade each with Jere Becker and Jim Riley. I'm indebted to both of them for helping to bring out the woman in me, teaching me that it's never too late. And Jere and Jim, each in his own ways, prepared me for another man who would bring me to full bloom.

My Best Love

The superlative in this chapter title defines the quality of the relationship I'm so fortunate to now have. Most people probably never experience such closeness, empathy, wonderment, and downright fun in the romantic company of another.

If I had been more superstitious, though, no doubt I would've deflected Cupid's arrow. The most meaningful men in my life had been Joe Neer, Jay, Jere Becker, Jim Riley, Joe Thompson, and Jack Kaufman—all men with first names beginning with J! How could I ever fit into my life and heart a man named David? The others had been important to me, to say the least, but when I met this man in 1995 I found my true soulmate. To repeat the dedication page of my last book, *Breaking Barriers*:

> For David Steinberg
> Journalist and gentle man
> Sine qua non

⁓

I had just finished a speaking engagement at the San Francisco Jewish Community Center a few years ago, and was autographing copies of my first book, *Dancing*

213

in the Dark. Susan Kroll, the contact person there, approached me and said that she knew David Steinberg who wrote a weekly column called "Seniorities" for the *San Francisco Examiner* (now the *San Francisco Chronicle)* who might be interested in reading my book.

"Good, Susan, send him a copy."

The following week, my phone rang and it was David Steinberg. He said, "This is a well written book. You've got a typo on page seventeen." After some chitchat, David asked with his characteristic frankness, "Are you cute?"

"How the hell would I know?" I answered. "I'm blind."

A couple of days later, my doorbell rang. It was David. After a minimum of pleasantries, he declared, "You *are* cute. I think I'll kiss you."

And he did. Whereupon, I met his boldness with the instruction, "Lower, please," and we both had our first laugh together. David held me gently at arm's length, looked at me, and said, "Frances Lief Neer, I don't know what you are, but you're the only one of it."

With that began the sharing of the most meaningful friendship of my life. David and I went to the RSVP Awards when he was honored for his years writing the "Seniorities" column in the *Examiner.* When he was awarded the North of Market Senior Center Award, I attended as his partner. I was by his side when he was honored at Senior Action Network. We've danced, gone to the theater, eaten out, and attended many parties. David has always been careful to introduce me to the people I couldn't see. We participated in his activities, my activities, and mutual activities. And with deepening resonance we participated in each other's personal

214

places, the secret places within our minds and hearts.

Through it all there have been joyful memories.

Early on in our relationship, David got into a cab and told the driver my address.

"Oh, I know where you're going."

"You do?" David responded with surprise.

"Yeah. Frances Neer's house. I used to take Jim Riley there all the time." David later told me he felt as if he'd ridden in the back seat of a cab with a ghost.

Once when I was with David at a Philharmonia Baroque Orchestra concert I introduced him to the woman sitting next to him. Not that I knew her, but that didn't matter. When she heard David's name she perked right up.

"Say... don't you write the 'Seniorities' column?"

"Yes I do."

"Then you can review this concert for the paper."

"No, I'm afraid not. That's someone else's assignment."

"You write about old people. Why not old music?"

As I introduce David to all and sundry, since I'm blind, David brings people to me. At one holiday season party he even brought over Hizzonor, the mayor. We immediately found a connection in that his sister is visually impaired.

At another holiday party John Evans handed David a pair of weird looking glasses.

"Here, put these on."

"Why? My eyes are two of the few things I have left that are still functional."

"So you always thought. Put these on and look at the Christmas tree." So David did.

"Now... feel more at home, Mr. Steinberg?"

Through these glasses the twinkling lights on the tree became—Stars of David!

Bill Gerrey, a good friend of mine from VIP, hosts a Groundhog Day party each year that brings together a lively crowd of merrymakers. It was my turn for once to introduce David around. When we were leaving, Bill said to him, "Goodnight, Mr. Frances."

Being blind is a condition, but not necessarily a prohibition. I do my best to ignore my physical self. The mind and spirit come first. That puts me in apparent disagreement with noted writer Edna St. Vincent Millay, who said something to the effect, "If the physical self is swell the rest of you can go to hell." I'll take my attitude over hers any day.

David has ceased being taken aback at how much his blind girlfriend gets out and about to meet people. David was soaking in the community Jacuzzi at his apartment house one night and a couple joined him. They were having a business conversation, and asked him, "What business are you in?"

"I write the 'Seniorities' column in the *Examiner*."

"Oh, we know who you are. David Steinberg. Frances has told us all about you." He struck up a conversation with them that lasted late into the night. I called and called him, worried that he wasn't home by his usual time. When he finally picked up the phone I didn't know whether to be mad at my overly loquacious journalist or merely relieved.

David and I use every opportunity to talk about each other to whomever when we're apart. I've said to him, "Please always talk about me when I'm gone." When I was in San Diego not long ago on a speaking engagement, I threw away my carefully composed

216

"sober" speech and talked instead about my adventures with David. I could tell people enjoyed hearing about this and was told later that I'd gotten a standing ovation. The second one in my life.

The first standing ovation had come many years before when I was teaching college. I had a new class of troubled ghetto teenagers who were entering freshmen. I showed them an art print and told them to write about it. A room full of puzzled, surly expressions, as if to say, "What does she want from us, anyway?" "Write what you see," I said. "Each one of you. Just what you see in the picture." And they did. Some wrote from the mind, about what was objectively depicted in the art. Others put down their emotional reactions to it. But they all wrote something about that picture. When I read their papers and told them that they had all done the assignment as I'd asked—"Good job, everybody!"—the class stood up and cheered. There's so much a little encouragement can do for those who are starved for it.

When we were first getting to know each other, warts and all, I must have said something disagreeable to David for he declared, "You're a vengeful person, Frances."

"No, I'm not. I'm sweet."

No comment was answer enough.

I called up my nephew Racetrack Fred in New York and asked him, "Am I sweet?"

I think I heard him stifle a laugh before answering. "No, you're tough—kind...but tough." So I called Fred's sister Shirley in Florida. "Am I sweet?" I asked.

"You're a lot of good things, Frances, but sweet ain't one of 'em."

I phoned Shirley's cousin Faith and her husband

Roy. "What do you think of me?" Tactful silence from Faith, but Roy said, "You're a tough old broad."

So I came back to David and said, "Okay, so I'm not sweet. But that doesn't make me vengeful." As I said in the preface to this book, I love my fellow man, even though there are some I really don't like. No matter what David may say about me in an angry moment he knows one truth about me as far as he's concerned: No woman is competition for me.

David's friends are theater people, fellow journalists, and activists on the senior scene. We share our friends with each other, such as Manfred Mackeben, a microbiologist whose articles appear in world-wide scientific journals, and Dean Goodman, an actor in local stage work for many, many years.

David and I talk on the phone many times each day. In the morning he'll say, "I want to hear your voice. It starts my day." That may launch us into a conversation or not. But one of us will call the other a little later to share some no doubt brilliant concept—or just to hear the sound of the other's voice.

Since I broke my hip our world has changed. Fewer escapades, but we've become even closer. He visits me one day each week and brings food. Potato salad, sandwiches, fresh fruit. And with food he brings something to read to me. That way, I see the world through David's eyes. Recently he read some Toni Morrison and we both resonated so with her inspired phrasing.

Sometimes David sings to me. One of his favorite songs is Rodgers and Hart's "My Funny Valentine" ("Don't change a hair for me, not if you care for me."). I've told him that I think the line is patronizing, but he insists that it's not. We may never resolve this difference

218

of opinion, but I still enjoy his singing this song. He also sings "Bewitched, Bothered, and Bewildered" ("I'm wild again, beguiled again, a simpering, whimpering child again.") David adds a few of his own variations to the lines, such as "Vexed again, perplexed again, and thanks to her I'm oversexed again.... Romance fini, chance fini, ants that invaded my pants fini..." Lorenz Hart would no doubt thrash in his grave at David's violation of his lyrics.

In one of his naughtier moods, David told me about an assignment he had in his early days as a reporter. He was to interview a group of strippers. The most renowned of these strip tease artists was an amazingly well-endowed young woman appropriately named Busty Brown. David said that when he was interviewing Ms. Brown her robe just happened to spread open to reveal her breasts.

"What did you do?" I asked him.

"These two monstrous melons just plunged out toward me. One of them hit me in the eye!"

"I know you, David. You just looked up open-mouthed, and whoops, you had a mouthful!"

In the first days of our courtship David would quote from Shakespeare's *Antony and Cleopatra*. "Age cannot wither her, nor custom stale her infinite variety. Most women cloy the appetites they feed. But she makes more hungry where most she satisfies." About the third time after he'd said that quote I asked him, "David, when you recite that should I be taking it personally?"

Coy as he can sometimes be, he didn't answer. He just left it up to me to believe or not that he felt about me as Antony felt about Cleo.

David has taught me critical reading, writing, and

listening. I like to think that I'm the only woman who truly understands—and experiences—David's essence. He's kind and a caregiver.

Sometimes we squabble. David claims that I can never tell a joke correctly. Once I was telling one to the cab driver taking us to the theater. David interrupted me. "No, you've got it all wrong!" He started to tell his version of the joke.

"Now, *you've* got it wrong," I came back at him.

We arrived at the theater with David and me still arguing over the proper telling of that joke. The cabbie never did hear the punch line.

Speaking of jokes, this is one that David and I got a kick out of.

A golfer was having a bad day on the course. Every drive he hit went off into the weeds, instead of down the fairway. So, he went into the rough retrieving his misdirected golf balls, putting them in one of his trouser pockets. He'd collected most of them when he was looking for one next to a road. An older woman happened to be walking her Pomeranian and saw the man. She stopped and stared at the bulging front pocket of his slacks. "What's that?" she asked.

"Golf balls," the man said dejectedly.

She considered his answer for a moment. "Is that anything like tennis elbow?"

As an older couple, David and I appreciated this one.

A sixty-year-old amateur artist was scrounging around in the attic of the home he and his wife had just moved into, when he found an old, strangely shaped bottle. The man wiped the dust from the bottle and—presto—a genie wafted out of it. As all gracious genies do, he offered to grant the man three wishes.

First, the man asked for an art show that would finally make him famous. Immediately, the man's cell phone rang. He answered it to find out that some of his work had been selected for an exhibition at the Guggenheim the following week.

Next, the man asked for his investments to flourish. His cell phone rang again. It was his broker telling him that all the man's stocks had split and they were going through the roof.

Fame and riches taken care of, the man carefully considered his last wish. "Mr. Genie," he said. "I'd like my wife to be thirty years younger than me."

In an instant, the man became ninety years old.

~

Here's no joke. David and I enjoy the fullness and roundness of sex. We have physical and emotional ESP. I'll spare any details, except to relate one of his loveliest compliments to me. "You've got an alabaster ass."

Once, at a Mills College graduation party, my sister-in-law Arlene met David. When she got back home to New York she phoned my nephew Bert's wife Luisita and said, "I've never known a man to love a woman as David loves Frances. He was so kind to her and careful of her."

That's my very deary Davey.

At this writing David is eighty-seven and I'm eighty-six. I'll never see his face, but clearly view his heart each hour of every day. Most important of all, what we share—and it's nothing less than magic—is that we help each other know who we are. And together we celebrate that knowledge. We're a laughing, crying, deeply understanding, just holding each other and loving it mutual appreciation society. We both enjoy the intricacies of literature and language, the essence of good writing, and the use of exactly the right word or turn of phrase. David helps me know the real me, and I do the same for him.

The other men in my life, each in different ways, had waited for me to serve them. And I obliged. Not until David was service a two-way street, a real give-and-take partnership. I'm happy to give to him, knowing that in the same moment David is preparing to give back.

Since I broke my hip, David and I don't go out much. But our relationship doesn't depend on that. He'll read to me from the *New York Times*, *New Yorker*, or *Newsweek*. He'll read me magazine articles that he's writing and ask for my input. It's all quality time with David. I wouldn't trade a minute of it for anything. There's not a doubt in my mind that if we had known each other as kids we would've argued, we would've scrapped, but we would've been together for good and all. For all that time we would've valued and supported each other's potentials, each other's abilities.

The beauty of David and me is also in our independence from each other. David has said, "We all have a secret room that nobody gets in. We're lucky if we're allowed to even approach the door to someone else's secret room." David and I feel safe at each other's door. But sometimes one of us will call the other and a word, a tone of voice, is enough to say, "You can't come in now." To know and be known like that is the most sublime treasure.

It's taken eighty years, but I'm finally no longer

alone in a crowd. David is there for me, and I for him. We protect, love, respect, and just plain enjoy each other. Surely the saddest fate a person can have is one self-imposed, commonly stated as, "It's too late for me." Not until I was old, blind, and physically compromised did David Steinberg come into my life. It just goes to show that we should never say that it's too late. If we're open to the magic of true love it can find us. And when that happens, we need to reach out with both hands and take hold of that magic. We must nurture and cherish this gift—never more so than in the autumn of our days.

> *Oh, it's a long, long while*
> *From May to December*
> *But the days grow short*
> *When you reach September.*
> *When the autumn weather*
> *Turns the leaves to flame,*
> *One hasn't got time*
> *For the waiting game.*
> *Oh, the days dwindle down*
> *To a precious few,*
> *September... November...*
> *And these few precious days*
> *I'll spend with you,*
> *These precious days*
> *I'll spend with you.**

* "September Song" (From the musical play "Knickerbocker Holiday") words by Maxwell Anderson, music by Kurt Weill

ISBN 141202526-5

9 781412 025263

596327